WORKING WITH ADOLE

BASIC TEXTS IN COUNSELLING AND PSYCHOTHERAPY

Series Editor: Stephen Frosh

This series introduces readers to the theory and practice of counselling and psychotherapy across a wide range of topic areas. The books will appeal to anyone wishing to use counselling and psychotherapeutic skills and will be particularly relevant to workers in health, education, social work and related settings. The books in this series are unusual in being rooted in psychodynamic and systemic ideas, yet being written at an accessible, readable and introductory level. Each text offers theoretical background and guidance for practice, with creative use of clinical examples.

Published

Jenny Altschuler
WORKING WITH CHRONIC ILLNESS

Bill Barnes, Sheila Ernst and Keith Hyde
AN INTRODUCTION TO GROUPWORK

Stephen Briggs
WORKING WITH ADOLESCENTS

Alex Coren
SHORT-TERM PSYCHOTHERAPY

Emilia Dowling and Gill Gorell Barnes
WORKING WITH CHILDREN AND PARENTS THROUGH
SEPARATION AND DIVORCE

Gill Gorell Barnes
FAMILY THERAPY IN CHANGING TIMES

Ravi Rana
COUNSELLING STUDENTS

Paul Terry
COUNSELLING THE ELDERLY AND THEIR CARERS

Jan Wiener and Mannie Sher
COUNSELLING AND PSYCHOTHERAPY IN PRIMARY HEALTH CARE

Invitation to authors

The Series Editor welcomes proposals for new books within the **Basic Texts in Counselling and Psychotherapy** series. These should be sent to Stephen Frosh at the School of Psychology, Birkbeck College, Malet Street, London, WC1E 7HX (email s.frosh@bbk.ac.uk).

Basic Texts in Counselling and Psychotherapy
Series Standing Order ISBN 0–333–69330–2
(*outside North America only*)

You can receive future titles in this series as they are published by placing a standing order. Please contact your bookseller or, in the case of difficulty, write to us at the address below with your name and address, the title of the series and the ISBN quoted above.

Customer Services Department, Macmillan Distribution Ltd
Houndmills, Basingstoke, Hampshire RG21 6XS, England

WORKING WITH ADOLESCENTS

A Contemporary Psychodynamic Approach

STEPHEN BRIGGS

First published 2002 by
PALGRAVE MACMILLAN
Houndmills, Basingstoke, Hampshire RG21 6XS and
175 Fifth Avenue, New York, N.Y. 10010
Companies and representatives throughout the world

PALGRAVE MACMILLAN is the global academic imprint of the Palgrave Macmillan division of St. Martin's Press, LLC and of Palgrave Macmillan Ltd. Macmillan® is a registered trademark in the United States, United Kingdom and other countries. Palgrave is a registered trademark in the European Union and other countries.

ISBN 0-333-94501-8

This book is printed on paper suitable for recycling and made from fully managed and sustained forest sources.

A catalogue record for this book is available from the British Library.

Library of Congress Cataloging-in-Publication Data

Briggs, Stephen.
  Working with adolescents : a contemporary psychodynamic approach / Stephen Briggs.
    p. cm. – (Basic texts in counselling and psychotherapy)
  Includes bibliographical references and index.
    ISBN 0–333–94501–8
    1. Adolescent psychotherapy. 2. Psychodynamic psychotherapy
I. Title. II. Series.

RJ505.P92 B75 2002
616.89′140835–dc21   2002025842

10   9   8   7   6   5   4   3   2   1
11 10 09 08 07 06 05 04 03 02

Printed in China

CONTENTS

ACKNOWLEDGEMENTS

The source of this book is the experience of working with adolescents and their families in the Adolescent Department of the Tavistock Clinic, and many teachers, colleagues and students have provided me with rich opportunities for thinking about adolescence. In particular I wish to thank Robin Anderson, Andrew Cooper, Anna Dartington, Helene Dubinsky, Louise Lyon, Deirdre Moylan, and Gianna Williams. I am grateful to the Psychosocial Studies group at the University of East London for the opportunities there to think about the meeting points of psychoanalytic and social theories. I am grateful to Stephen Frosh for his helpful editing. I wish also to acknowledge the many young people I have worked with, and who formed the basis for the case examples used in the book. All case material is disguised and fictionalised in order to preserve confidentiality and anonymity. Finally, I wish to thank Beverley and Eleanor for their support and patience while I was writing.

STEPHEN BRIGGS

FOREWORD

In the last fifty years adolescence has forced its way into the consciousness of western society, provoking anxiety, excitement and envy by turns in the older generation. While many of these reactions say more about the adults than the adolescents themselves, any serious student of adolescence can see that many of our young people are in deep trouble. This is witnessed by the increase in male adolescent suicides, or of young drug addicts, or the record levels of delinquency and violence in which young people are both perpetrators and victims.

Some of the tasks of adolescence captured by Stephen Briggs in Chapter 9 on leaving home – becoming a parent, becoming a student, becoming a worker, becoming a sexual partner – are now much more difficult in a world which is so complex and so rapidly changing. Young people do not have the bedrock of adult certainty to challenge and accommodate to since most adults are themselves having to cope with such different circumstances from the situation of their own adolescence. For example, most jobs that young people are starting did not exist in their parents' generation and the jobs their parents had have disappeared. Gone are the days of following in the footsteps of parents. Thus the notion of a role model cannot be anything like as concrete as it once was. All the different aspects of becoming an adult require of young people a much deeper working through of the tasks of adolescence in the context of parents – so vital for the support of young people – who find it much harder to contain them. In other words, it is very hard to help young people through a process which is so bewildering and anxiety-provoking for the adults themselves.

The challenge for professionals trying to help young people in trouble is clear. Society is slowly recognising that something needs to be done, but often professionals are thrust into tasks of helping young people only to find themselves faced with situations which are hard to understand and therefore hard to find ways of being constructive.

In order to deal with this, Stephen Briggs has produced a rather unique guidebook. The reader will find here a wealth of information on young people and how to go about trying to help them. His psychodynamic approach allows the reader a way of describing and understanding their deepest fears and conflicts. What he then does is to show how these fears interact with the complexities of the external lives of young people. How do they form a new more adult identity? Briggs sees adolescent identity as being formed out of relationships – it is for him an interpersonal identity. He plots through adolescent development how their sense of subjectivity gradually changes, including the complexity of being part of a multi-ethnic society, which he explores through the experiences of teenagers from different ethnic backgrounds. The need to find ways of managing this particular task must, especially now, be one of the most important of all.

The question of parenting and working with adolescents and their impact on institutions takes us back to the problem that professionals have in working with adolescents. Young people can get 'under our skin' and we find ourselves full of and often paralysed by the very feelings which the young people cannot deal with. Briggs shows how this can be understood as the imparting of feeling – the projection – into those who are trying to care for them. Often these experiences are unpleasant and alarming as well as frustrating but when we can understand the process then at least the struggle can be seen as relevant and helpful in our attempts to come alongside young people and help them find their lost hope and courage.

Adolescence is an odyssey which requires courage and a capacity to face loneliness, and many cannot manage this alone. In *Working with Adolescents* Stephen Briggs helps readers to help young people to resume this journey when they have lost their way, or given up altogether. It will sustain professionals in their efforts to struggle with the young people they are trying to help.

ROBIN ANDERSON
Member of the British Psychoanalytic Society
Consultant Psychiatrist
Former Chair of the Adolescent Department
Tavistock Clinic

INTRODUCTION

Primarily, this book aims to provide an understanding of adolescence to the wide range of professionals who work with adolescents, and it is written to be relevant to those who are engaging with and thinking therapeutically about adolescents. It aims, therefore, to be relevant to professionals from the wide range of disciplines who have roles in working with adolescents, either as a part of their working lives or within agencies which specialise in work with adolescents. It aims to be relevant to professionals who are relatively new to psychotherapeutic concepts and methods, and also to those who may have this kind of experience, but who wish to know more about working with adolescents.

Many more professionals in more settings – traditional clinics, community therapeutic services, schools, GP practices, youth work, social work, youth justice, and nursing, in both community and inpatient settings – are required to take an increasing role in providing adolescent therapy and to develop skills in working with adolescents. An adolescent may be offered and accept an appointment to meet a therapist in a clinic, after a considered process of referral, or, more spontaneously, s/he may telephone or 'drop in' to a community-based therapy or counselling centre. Therapeutic work also takes place when an adolescent initiates or takes up an offer to talk in more detail about a personal, emotional or relational situation to a teacher, youth worker or social worker. Whether the contact is formal or informal, individual or in a group or family setting, the dynamics of the meeting, between adolescent and adult, have distinctive qualities. I have in mind a sense of therapeutic consultation taking place in all these settings, by all these professionals, and define therapeutic consultation as making a contact with an adolescent with a therapeutic task in mind, or with a therapeutic mind turned to the task; both of these. I also have in mind more formal, intensive and long-term therapy with adolescents which is made distinctive by the nature of adolescence.

One of the difficulties professionals have to encounter in work with adolescents is that the social context is subject to rapid changes. In recent times, the pace of change has accelerated, creating new conditions of diversity and uncertainty. Late adolescence in particular has been subject to a radical social restructuring, so that new psychological problems follow in the wake of these changes (Coleman and Hendry 1999). There is in effect an overlapping of the new and the traditional. Some traditional key aspects of adolescent development remain crucial – the experiences of developing sexuality through the impact of puberty, separation from childhood ways of relating to parental figures, and a quest for a sense of identity, to name three – but the meaning and configuration of these now are radically different, and diverse.

Thus, there are new contexts for adolescence, which are characterised by diversity. The development of an identity in adolescence is radically affected by these changes, so that growing from childhood into adulthood – a process now taking longer – constitutes a deep engagement with loss, in a context of uncertainty, ambiguity and anxiety. Theories for working therapeutically with adolescence need to fit the socio-cultural scene of contemporary society, rather than, as is still the case, the cultures of the mid twentieth century. Psychotherapeutic theories and techniques have also changed and there is a need to apply these to adolescence, so that thinking about the contemporary context of adolescence is matched with current theories of therapeutic relating and intervening. Psychotherapeutic work with adolescence in contemporary contexts is under-theorised.

Thus this book addresses these issues. Chapter 1 discusses the particular kinds of turbulence that affect adolescents, especially the new risks and hazards of adolescence, and recent thinking that identity is formed in and through relationships, rather than through a solitary withdrawal from others. The discussion of identity is developed further in Chapter 2, where the concept of 'subjectivation', the process of becoming a subject, is applied to understanding unfolding identity in adolescence, through the development of the capacity to think one's own thoughts, and to own one's own body and passions. There is a particular emphasis on the way adolescents move between 'positions', reflecting emotional states and relatedness to others, rather than in a uniform linear progression from childhood towards adulthood. Chapter 3 focuses on the diversity of identities through a discussion of ethnic identity, and the importance of relating a multicultural context of difference to work with adolescents. Chapters 4 and 5 explore relationships between adolescents and parents, carers and professionals in organisations. Chapters 6 and 7 develop the idea of outsidership, and relates this to some of the main problems of adolescents that professional workers have to face – eating disorders, delinquency, drug use – and there is attention given here to adolescents with disabilities. Chapter 8 focuses on extreme difficulties, psychosis and suicide. In Chapter 9, the changes in the adolescent process are reflected by the way that routes into adulthood are more complex and often deferred. The traditional way of conceptualising this process is through thinking about leaving home; here the suggestion is that adolescents take up roles of becoming more adult, in a piecemeal and uncertain transition into adulthood.

The conceptual framework needed to understand these issues is complex, and the aim is to discuss this clearly and straightforwardly, without denying real complexities. The main orientation is a psychoanalytic framework, from which I draw especially on contemporary influences, particularly from the school of object relations. The key concepts in this approach are explained, discussed and applied to case examples. Second, adolescence is thought of as a psycho-social concept, and adolescents develop within contexts in which internal and interpersonal – or intersubjective – processes are in interaction with, influencing and influenced by, the social and cultural worlds. Thus the discussion introduces and illustrates contemporary social thinking which makes sense of current adolescent issues, conflicts and difficulties.

Adolescence, perhaps by definition, always seems to be in crisis. From the complaint of a shepherd in Shakespeare's *The Winter's Tale* that

> I would there were no age between ten and three-and- twenty, or that youth would sleep out the rest, for there is nothing in the between but getting wenches with child, wronging the ancientry, stealing, fighting

through the images of rebellious mid-twentieth-century youth to contemporary 'folk devils' (Cohen 1973), there is concern about sexually and violently dangerous adolescents. Concerns about suicide, self-harm, substance misuse, offending behaviour, depression and eating disorders among disadvantaged, disaffected, dangerous and self-destructive youth focus the attention of an increasingly large number of professionals who aim to help young people who are in difficulties, and their families and networks; such concerns and attention are backed by increasing evidence that problems in adolescence do not just wither away, but are indicators of future adult difficulties. Engagement with adolescent difficulties is crucial, and difficult. In emphasising the importance of developing a reflective space for thinking about the impact of adolescent emotionality, the book aims to equip professionals to understand adolescents, and themselves in relation to adolescents, so that more effective therapeutic contact can be achieved. Thus, very practically, the book addresses the problem that concerns so many of those who belong to services working with adolescents, namely, how to make and sustain therapeutic contact with vulnerable adolescents whose need for therapeutic help is urgent, and who, if not helped, are vulnerable to experiencing long–lasting difficulties.

Adolescence is a momentous time. The changes that take place and the experiences of getting to know oneself, and others, while developing a sense of a complex identity and place in the world, bring anxieties, vulnerabilities, opportunities and much to think about. Professionals' also working with adolescents, have a lot to think about, and it is hoped this book will stimulate thinking as well as providing guidance in the exacting but rewarding endeavour of working with adolescents.

CONTEMPORARY ADOLESCENCE: TURBULENCE OR TRANSITION?

This chapter explores the context of contemporary adolescence and focuses on the qualities of turbulence, internal and external, that affect adolescents during the transition from childhood to adulthood. The discussion then addresses how the social context affects the adolescent quest for identity, and the ways thinking about identity is now more focused on relationships. Consideration of the risks, hazards and opportunities of contemporary adolescence leads, in particular, to the exploration of the potential for fragmentation of identity. Bion's theory of container–contained is applied to thinking about ways in which these anxieties of contemporary adolescence can be understood and addressed.

Turbulence or transition: a question of (adult) ideology?

Case example: Maria

Maria requested a therapeutic consultation when she was 21, because feeling depressed and having a lack of confidence in herself increasingly troubled her. In her consultation, Maria was very tearful, and said that she felt 'stupid' for being so easily moved to tears. She felt she should be stronger, but that she was 'pathetic'. She said she was very close to her parents, especially her mother, with whom 'she could talk about almost anything'. Her mixed-race parents got on OK too, though they had had some difficulties when she was younger, when they had argued a lot about her older half-brother, her mother's son.

Maria said her adolescence had not been particularly difficult or traumatic. There had been very little conflict between her and her parents. She had got on well at school, had progressed to university, and she was nearing the end of her course. She had many friends, enjoyed a 'going out' lifestyle, and she had boyfriends. One of these had been serious for a time, but though she was still keen on him, he wanted 'some space'. Now, in comparison with her teens she was 'very up and down', and she described within herself feeling 'wobbly, not at all solid'. She felt others around her were more secure and more confident. Her brother in particular 'made her feel stupid'. He and his friends could talk about things – like chaos theory and complexity – but she felt she had nothing to say. She wished she could talk like them. She felt she ought to be more independent, especially that she ought to be more sep-arate from her mother, but she did not like being alone and she did not know what she wanted to do in the future.

Maria's situation illustrates some of the key features that need to be taken into account in thinking about contemporary adolescence. She lives in a mixed-race reconstituted family and lives at home while going to university. She is asking for thera-peutic help at the age of 21 when, in traditional terms, she should be considered 'adult' rather than 'adolescent'. She is depressed, uncertain why, and comments on the closeness and openness of her relationship with her mother and her lack of conflict in her teens.

Maria's is one narrative about adolescence, and one of the most striking features of adolescence – and thinking about ado-lescence – is diversity. There are accounts which stress that ado-lescence is a time of turbulence, which comes out all right in the end – somehow:

> While this is a time of turbulence, disturbance and struggle, often of inner uncertainties and chaos, the adolescent's growing discovery of his [sic] own sexually maturing body and physical strength, alongside his developing mind and intellect, usually enables him to move from depen-dence to independence. (Wise 2000 p. 7)

On the other hand, there are concerns that the risks and hazards to which adolescents are exposed leave them vulnerable to the development of psycho-social disorders, which peak during the adolescent years. Suicide, self-harm, substance misuse, offend-ing behaviour, depression and eating disorders are among the risks. These problems, rather than being grown out of, can, if untreated, persist into adulthood and have detrimental effects on adult functioning (Smith and Rutter 1995; Graham 1986; Achenbach *et al.* 1998):

> The mental health of young people is enormously vulnerable because of the many, diverse challenges they face in adolescence and also because of a propensity to engage in at-risk behaviour. Some young people are also exposed to harmful circumstances which affect their mental health . . . Singly or more usually in combination, these at-risk behaviours and adverse circumstances increase the vulnerability of young people to psychosocial disorders. Graham (1986) estimated the overall prevalence of mental health problems in the adolescent population at 20 per cent with 7 to 10 per cent having moderate to severe problems. (Baruch 2001 p. 3)

Maria's depression, her tearfulness and her feelings of low self-worth – as she puts it, feeling 'pathetic' and 'stupid' – seem central to her difficulties. Do they indicate vulnerability to longer-term problems, or are they responses to the process of change and transition she is encountering?

Some adolescents find that the social transitions expected of them are overwhelming. Both the transition into adolescence from childhood, which requires entering puberty and, usually, changing schools, and the late adolescent transition into adulthood create conditions of uncertainty and change. Maria can be identified as someone who is experiencing anxiety about the late adolescent transition, but who, in reporting that her teenage years were not particularly full of conflict, seems to fit with the view that

> There is little evidence to support the notion of wide ranging conflict between the generations . . . findings from research are unequivocal. Serious conflict between parents and adolescents is true only of a small minority of families, which should bring some comfort to those parents who contemplate the onset of adolescence with trepidation. (Coleman and Hendry 1999 p. 80)

Some adolescents, it is argued, make a smooth transition through adolescence while others have a more stressful and turbulent experience. Parents and teenagers, like Maria and her mother, can remain connected to each other rather than becoming estranged. They can spend as much time together in adolescence as in earlier childhood and, although adolescents spend less time in total in the family than younger children, there can be a compensating sense of increased communication between them and their parents. Since adolescence is usually defined as turbulent, it can come as a surprise that some accounts of adolescence refer to the continuity of relationships between parents and adolescents, the absence of communication breakdown with parents, the absence of symptoms of psychological distress and difficulty in relation to peers and adults (Coleman and Hendry 1999, p. 209). Turmoil may be located in a minority of adolescents – a highly significant minority from the point of professional practice, since these are more likely to be the adolescents who are encountered by professionals.

These accounts caution against a normative approach to adolescence in which turmoil is assumed to be universal. In fact, turmoil may be thought of as denoting a particular social construction of adolescence, and therefore an adult-centred approach (Roche and Tucker 1997). As Van Heeswyk points out, the 'stormy' view of adolescence 'is the theory that underpins the commercial exploitation of young people' (1997 p. 29), who are characteristically represented as 'inherently deviant or deficient' or, more specifically,

> presented as either actively deviant or passively at risk and sometimes as both simultaneously. In general young men are more likely to be presented as actively deviant, especially in aggressive forms and especially if they are working class and/or black. Young women are more likely to be constructed as passively at risk. (Griffin 1997 p. 18)

From this perspective, it is not just individual differences that determine whether adolescence is turbulent or proceeds in a smooth transition to adulthood, but the social context in which some groups are more vulnerable than others, especially in terms of race, gender, class and sexuality. The contextual differences of individuals, and the availability of resources, primarily in the form of reliable and trustworthy relationships with adults, may be extremely significant in whether adolescents succumb to the impact of the transition, with a consequent risk to long-term mental health.

Psychoanalytic thinking about adolescence has provided detailed understanding of the impact of the bodily changes of puberty. These changes are multifaceted and provide a focus for the origins of turbulence. Melanie Klein (1922) wrote of 'the tempestuous uprush of instincts arising at puberty' (p. 56). Peter Blos (1962, 1967) discussed the eruption of infantile feelings as the pubertal adolescent experiences a crisis of separating from childhood ways of relating to parents. Now, faced with the emergence of an adult body, the adolescent identifies with the same-sex parent, and with emergent adult sexual and parenting potentiality. That is, s/he may, with this body, one day become a mother or father. Traditionally, the perspective these theories take is triangular, or oedipal.[1] Powerful passions are stirred up and revived in the adolescent, including desire for and competition with parents. The passions of childhood take place, in adolescence, in a context in which the new physical capacities of the adolescent make such wishes potentially realisable. Taking the boy's relationship with the father, Anderson discusses the shift in power from childhood to adolescence as relative to the parent, and as potentially destabilising:

> It is the very balance of a relatively weak child and relatively strong parents which, whatever the impulses and anxieties, is a background bedrock of reality which allows for a sense of safety. In adolescence the situation is extremely different. The boy is suddenly quite strong, and with more cognitive capacity, and he could kill his father if he did not prevent himself, and yet the impulse is just as strong. (Anderson 1999 p. xvii)

Turbulence thus resides in the processes originating with the experience of puberty, and the strength of passionately felt emotions which emerge, or revive. In the face of these passionate trends, relationships with parents are unbalanced, forcing a reorganisation or renegotiation of these relationships. Depending on the perspective, psychoanalytic accounts focus on separating, identifying and the loss of childhood relationships. These accounts also emphasise the importance of anxiety, feeling vulnerable and, through the increase in physical and cognitive capacity, an emergent sense of power. This is especially thought of as the power to act, which in both sexual and aggressive aspects can feel both liberating and frightening. These terms – anxiety, vulnerability and power – are very important ones in thinking about adolescence.

Thus central psychoanalytic ideas about adolescence, that it is a turbulent time which places tremendous stress on the adolescent, contrast diametrically with the idea of smooth transition, which usually emanate from a more academic psychology or sociology. Perhaps these differences represent incompatible approaches – Van Heeswyk (1997 p. 29) suggests that psychoanalysts have had more fun! From the perspective which locates turbulence in a small but vulnerable section of adolescents emerges the accusation that psychoanalytic theories have generalised, mistakenly, from the pathological. On the other hand, those accounts which emphasise smooth transitions are often based on self-report rather than contemporary clinical accounts, and may tend to emphasise coping rather than feeling overwhelmed. Many accounts point out that the miserable, abject and difficult aspects of adolescence are 'forgotten' by adults (Jacobs 1990, Griffin 1997, Sayers 1991). These disowned aspects of having a more turbulent time of it in adolescence are then projected back on to adolescents by adults, who do not wish to know about the feelings they themselves experienced in adolescence.

Jacobs (1990) discusses how memories of adolescence tend to be split between idealisation of moments of success, achievement and energy and those which are abject and miserable. He thinks that early adolescence embodies the latter and late adolescence the former:

> early adolescence . . . is 'a time of awkwardness, of disproportions, of frightening sexual maturation, of pimples, and of new and untried feelings. Nothing is set. Nothing is solid. Everything is in flux and change.' The aim with early adolescence, is to get past it and then, not to look back. In contrast, late adolescence is idealised, especially as future experiences include disappointments and frustrations. (p. 109)

Sayers (1991) interviewed adults who had either 'forgotten' their adolescence or who recalled it as a nightmare. She quotes Andre Green saying:

> We outgrow adolescence with the idea of having lived through an exalting moment that we will never forget, but, in reality, sometimes when we look back we realize we had a narrow escape. (Green 1992)

Whether Maria has been more affected by puberty than she says, and whether she is putting the misery of her earlier adolescence out of mind, can only be discovered by further exploration with her. She does say that she feels wobbly, not solid inside, and that compared with others, such as her brother, she questions the strength of her own mind, and the capacity to commit herself to expressing her own thoughts. She is uncertain in her identity.

Psycho-social perspectives on adolescence

The evidence of high vulnerability to psycho-social disorder in adolescence, and the complexity of the factors associated with risk, indicate that there is a need to connect psychoanalytic views about internal turbulence with the contexts in which adolescents experience stressful transition. The psycho-social approach to adolescence in which the internal and individual quest for identity is linked with society and culture has developed out of Erikson's work, and this can be briefly explored to provide a foundation for thinking about the interplay of individual psychological experiences of adolescence and the social context.

Erikson (1968) emphasised the importance of the social environment in harnessing or frustrating adolescent energy and vitality. He proposed a close fit between the possibilities available to adolescents in society, and the achievement of a sense of transition through adolescence, to successful adulthood. On the other hand, if the environment was felt to restrict the adolescent, 'role confusion' was the consequence. For Erikson this was not a matter of nicety, or luxury, but it really mattered. Identity was essential for psychic survival, for 'there is no feeling of being alive without a sense of identity' (Erikson 1968 p. 129).

Erikson, as Noam (1999) points out, was an outsider himself[2] and this may have some bearing on why he believed identity to be such a serious issue, a 'fateful process that enhanced or decreased the chances of survival' (Noam p. 50). Survival involved choice, morality, ideology and future orientation. Erikson located developing the capacity to contend with these life-essential decision-making processes in adolescence.

Developing an identity means separating from others, becoming an individual and gaining a sense of self and other. The concept of identity is thus a cousin, so to speak, of Blos's separating–individuating adolescent, which is discussed below (Chapter 2). The adolescent has to distinguish between self and others through formulating answers to the questions 'Who am I and who am I like? And also who am I not?' The search for identity takes place in a psycho-social matrix, forced upon the adolescent by the impact of puberty from within and the social contexts, demands and rituals from the outside.

Erikson postulated that, though it may differ in nature, timing and duration, societies provide a space for the 'playful' consolidation of identity, before this is called upon to provide the adult with the necessary equipment for survival. Erikson called the time of consolidation a 'psychosocial moratorium'. In social and cultural contexts where there is more emphasis on individuality the moratorium will be longer, and vice versa. Thus like Blos he thought of Western society as incorporating a prolonged adolescence. Where the outcome of adolescence – that is, the nature of the transition to adulthood – is more prescribed collectively, in terms of work role and work or career expectations and sexual partnerships, the process of identity exploration will be foreclosed. In societies where there is prolonged adolescence, individuals may experience intense anxiety under the pressure of which they may also 'foreclose' on the process of suspending commitment, or the exploration of desire. On the other hand, anxiety about the indeterminate state of adolescence can lead to acting-out, to the development of patterns of delinquency, promiscuity and so on, which become fixed as antisocial or self-destructive patterns of relating and behaving. The aim in the adolescent moratorium is to suspend commitment and to explore, through experiencing confusion and uncertainty, out of which a sense of similarity to and difference from parents can emerge.

The pressure on the adolescent in the adolescent moratorium can be intense. The adolescent can be in a pained state, and 'is apt to suffer more deeply than he ever did before or ever will again from a confusion of roles' (Erikson 1968 p. 167). Under these tensions, there are conflicting pressures either to regress or to attempt to foreclose the quest for identity. However, the test of identity is the commitment to and engagement with intimacy; 'only an attempt to engage in intimate fellowship and competition or in sexual intimacy fully reveals the latent weakness of identity' (Erikson 1968 p. 167).

There is thus a two-phased conceptualisation. First, the adolescent withdraws from commitment in order to delay an entry to adulthood and to reconfigure the inner world; second, there is the test of commitment, which is undertaken through the exercise of choice and the immersion in an intimate relationship. This demonstrates, through the capacity of the individual to become involved and remain true to the self, whether the identity, which has been forged in the moratorium, will stand the test of application to the reallife tasks of adulthood.

Erikson's work on identity underpins contemporary thinking about adolescence. On the other hand, this model of adolescence is restrictive and probably outmoded by the recent emergence of different ways of thinking about relationships. Erikson has been criticised specifically for focusing on individualism, autonomy and achievement through his antipathy towards collectives (Sayers 1991), rather than paying attention to the importance of relationships (Noam 1999), and thus being predominantly 'masculine' and diminishing femininity in his approach.[3] The essential mechanism of a 'fit' or 'misfit' between the individual and the culture, which varies from time and place, is a flexible and adaptable one. However, the conceptualisation of the outcome is far too solid and unitary for the experience of modernity, which is characterised by unpredictability and uncertainty. In other words, Erikson had a rather stable view of societies. Even as he was conceiving *Identity: Youth and Crisis*, Emery and Trist (1969) were formulating ideas about turbulent systems, in which 'dynamic properties arise not simply from the field itself. The "ground" is in motion', and this leads to increasing uncertainty (p. 249). In modernity, all that is solid melts into air.

Turbulence and risks

One way of thinking about the qualitative psychosocial changes since Erikson formulated his ideas about identity is to adapt Roberts's (1995) well-used metaphor of train and car journeys. Roberts suggests that adolescence used to be like a train journey. The route was predictable and the destination pre-arranged. It was possible to travel together with others and develop a sense of cohesion, community and camaraderie with them, sharing the same route and aiming for the destination. Though there were possibilities of changing route, these could be made only at planned stops.

In contrast, contemporary adolescence is more like a car journey. There is an appearance of freedom and autonomy over the journey compared with trains, and a sense of control over the choice of routes and destination through the individual driver constantly making a series of individual decisions. There is much less of a collective sense of travelling together in a car, though 'virtual' contact can be maintained with others by radio, stereo, mobile phone and even on-board internet connection.

The train journey is rather like Erikson's model of identity, where the journey provides the moratorium. The predictability of the train journey is replaced by the confusing image of the car journey, which provides a semblance or illusion of control and independence, but unequal opportunities (some start the car journey in a Porsche!), and greater responsibility for decision-making and isolation from others. In the car journey the problem is about joining with others as well as separating from them. Additionally, the car journey confronts the driver with a set of unpredictable risks.

Martin (1981) has argued that the first wave of adolescence in the mid twentieth century followed the rise in teenage spending power and the spread of rock music, with images and a language of unconventionality, strongly supported and transmitted through media. The second wave of adolescence in the late twentieth and early twenty-first centuries is characterised by globalisation, consumerism, and the invasion of 'space' by increasing numbers and intensities of images and the increasing fragmentation. Frosh (1991) characterises this as: 'This babble – the constant speech of mass media and computer, all different, all distorted – produces a set of competing discourses that are experienced subjectively as mysterious and confusing, but yet are constitutive of our consciousness of the world' (p. 58), and which lead to 'incomprehension and misrecognition' so that the 'fragmentation of the cultural environment becomes a buzzing and booming confusion in the head' (p. 188).

The impact of modernity and post-modernity has been surprisingly undocumented with regard to adolescence, though it seems probable that there are an upside and a downside for young people, as there are for adults (Frosh 1991).

Perhaps the effect is to blur the distinction between adolescence and adulthood, through creating a context for adulthood which is distinctly 'adolescent', with an 'upside' which provides a sense of excitement and the thrill of new possibilities, alongside a questioning or deconstruction of old certainties. In this lie great possibilities for rethinking relationships, for overthrowing old prejudices, and for 'individualisation' (Beck 1992), subjectively or objectively feeling free of the old, constraining structures of thought and action. On the 'downside' there is an exposure to the fragmentation of the cultural environment and to new risks. In the absence of a bedrock of certainty and predictability, anxiety and a fear of loss of control are heightened. There is in this sense an encounter with loss – loss of a sense of a centre and of a past in which there are certainties of tradition. Whether excitement and thrill or a sense of loss and a fear of loss of control are uppermost, these are essential reactions to the changes of modernity, and mirror the movement from latency to adolescence. The loss of the 'bedrock' of certainty means that everyone is in the process of 'leaving home', or – to mix the developmental analogy – it is not only God who ceases to exist, but also latency, the intermission of certainty, reliability and predictability, which are sidelined to the periphery of 'anorak' activities such as collecting stamps and pricing antiques.

Adolescents have not simply to deal with the problem of leaving childhood certainties and dependencies, but also to gain a way of relating to adult post-modern adolescence. This means encountering turbulence in the socio-cultural context and the fluctuating, shifting, rapidly changing and uncertain adult world. It means moving into an adult world, which is extremely diverse and definable in many different ways. Two themes which emerge from this analysis and which are extremely important for contemporary adolescence are, first, the experience of loss and the importance and difficulty of mourning, and, second, fear of loss of control. The anxieties and defences that are brought about by both these issues are important to a consideration of adolescent identity development in conditions of turbulence.

Identity crisis

At this point we can return to Maria's predicament. She is facing an uncertain future, not knowing what she wants to do. In terms of her identity she feels wobbly and unable to make commitments. She is close to her mother, but the process of separating from her and finding her own mind has probably not taken place. She finds she cannot join in discussions and thus feels ill equipped to enter social relationships. It is probable that she has not been able to work out her rivalry with her brother, and his with her. The context of this is an uncertain future in a complex society. Appropriately, she says that she cannot talk about chaos theory and complexity!

It is possible when working with adolescents to notice 'Eriksonian' identity conflicts and struggles, as adolescents seek direction and aim to test commitments. They may also pull back from commitment, appropriately, because it feels too early, or like foreclosing. They may communicate a sense of being in flux. On the other hand, it is often the case that the withdrawal into an identity–forming moratorium indicates a defensive withdrawal from relationships, and the idealisation of the past, indicating a difficulty in undertaking internally the process of mourning that is needed in order to relinquish childhood.

Isolation and lack of engagement

Case example: Bill

Bill, an 18-year-old, maintained that he could not commit himself to knowing what path to take in his life because he had no way of knowing what he wanted to do, or what would be best for him. He proposed this as an existential dilemma, that since the aim of life was death, there was little point in choosing any particular form of engagement. This stance meant that he pulled back from relationships and spent very long periods of time on his own. Yet behind this rationalisation lay a very painful predicament in which he felt he had to cover up a sense of failure. He saw himself as very bright and yet he had the greatest difficulty in applying himself to his studies. Rather than engage with frustrations, he withdrew to 'start over again', saying he needs 'time out'. On one occasion he failed an exam and he was completely devastated. He felt it was all downhill from childhood, in which he idealised himself as a little boy Bill who was 'good at everything'. He felt he could still 'do anything' and he compared himself to David Beckham, who had simply had a lucky break. Idealisation of the past was supported by his grandiosities. His fear that he was 'losing it' constituted a crisis of loss and a fear of loss of control.

Distress in intimacy

Case example: Kirsty

Kirsty, also 18, had a boyfriend and the relationship had become fairly serious. At first she hoped it would be more successful than her previous relationships, which had been very short-lived, but eventually the relationship began to fall apart in mutual recriminations and hurt. Kirsty felt unable to be with her boyfriend without feeling extremely pained, jealous, suspicious and furious, and also she was quite incapable of spending any time apart from him without experiencing intense loneliness. In an overwhelmed and distressed state she stopped seeing him and said she wanted a life without commitment, where she felt free. Kirsty oscillated between feeling overwhelmed when involved, and lonely when withdrawing from others.

In both these examples the 'identity crisis' was centrally about a difficulty encountered in making and sustaining contact with others. In slightly different ways, both Bill and Kirsty experienced a need to withdraw from contact with others through difficulties in regulating or managing the emotional impact of contact. In both cases there was a sense of loss involved in the experience of engagement, and both withdrew from attempting to manage intense feelings to idealisations of states where this was not felt to be so urgent. Both experienced a loss of control through engagement, through becoming overwhelmed by the emotions that were thus generated.

Vulnerability and risk

Both Bill and Kirsty were clearly vulnerable young people. Adolescents are vulnerable especially if there have been adverse circumstances in early childhood (Smith and Rutter 1995). Vulnerability means having a propensity to feel hurt or wounded, a lack of self-confidence and/or a fragility or brittleness. It may also be indicated by a carefulness in relating – being careful, that is, with regard to how one relates to others (Dale 1991). Vulnerability is the antithesis of robustness and resilience. In the face of anxiety some characteristic defences of adolescence are activated. These include closure of the wish (or need) to make contact with others, taking flight, acting, and becoming oppositional, manic and omnipotent.

The vulnerable adolescent then experiences the context of engaging in the social world, through making relationships and engagement in work or study, as holding potential risks to the self. Risks of a psycho-social nature are unequally distributed throughout society so that some individuals are more exposed to being vulnerable. Adolescents are a vulnerable group (Rutter and Smith 1995). Current psychosocial risks include threats to mental health, which are evidenced in concerns about suicide, eating disorders, depression and antisocial behaviour. This makes adolescence 'a window of risk' (Furlong and Cartmel 1997). Risks may be thought of as involving increasingly individualised sets of decisions in an uncertain social context. 'As individuals are made to feel more responsible for life-events, uncertainty and risk have taken their toll on young people's mental health' (Furlong and Cartmel 1997 p. 9). Separating and joining or connecting (or reconnecting) with others attract risks.

Facing unknowns can only be assessed in terms of probabilities. The exposure to risk assessment, and to actual hazards, creates a climate in which anxiety, uncertainty and ambiguity have cumulative effects on the individual, leading either to the adoption of risk-taking behaviour as a way of life or to defences against the existence of risks. Some kinds of sexual, aggressive or antisocial behaviour are thought of, normatively, as constituting risk. On the other hand, aiming to eradicate risks provides an illusion of safety. Bill and Theresa can be thought of as withdrawing, not into an identity-forming moratorium, but into defensive illusions of safety which are outside any commitment to engagement.

Much debate has attended the meaning of the actual social changes that impact upon adolescents and their effects in terms of enhancing risks. The transition through late adolescence has become an extended one, in which unclear pathways to adulthood, diverse routes through adolescence and potential fragmentation of the process to adulthood have come to predominate (Furlong and Cartmel 1997). Above all, the sequences of transition from adolescence to adulthood are diverse and unpredictable. In fact they have become 'desequenced'[4] (Smith and Rutter 1995).

Turbulence and containment

Case example: Howard

Howard at 21, when he was referred for psychotherapy, was an example of someone in a late, deferred transition from adolescence to adulthood. He was in his last year at university and it was at this point in his life that he experienced 'role confusion'.

He arrived about thirty minutes late for the first appointment, and came into the consulting room tightly clutching a piece of paper, which I saw was his appointment letter. Looking tense, he sat down without taking off his coat and apologised for being late, in a way which suggested he was making a great effort to be offhand, or 'cool'. He had an air of self-deprecation, which continued when he told me he really did not know why he was here. His doctor had suggested he came, because he kept 'going mad when I get drunk'. He said he did not think he was a priority – as many other people might have more need of counselling.

He then told me something of himself, his family and his earlier adolescence.

His teens, he said, had not been particularly 'turbulent', though his mother had been ill and father was away at work a great deal. His older brother and sister had been much more in need of parental attention, and he had 'got on with it' completing his schooling, taking a gap year to 'get away from it all' and then going to university. Now, however, he was in constant conflict with his mother, whom he felt favoured his siblings, and his father was 'as useless as a hole in the head'. This description could have been applied to himself, for when he described what it meant to 'go mad when I get drunk' he told me about times, which he subsequently could not remember, in which he became violent towards others and put himself at risk, in ways which suggested he was not able to think about protecting himself.

Young people, like anyone else, can be very anxious at the prospect of having a therapeutic consultation, and this seemed to be prominent in the way Howard started this meeting. He was palpably anxious, and his lateness and tension, the way he clutched the letter communicated this. He was trying on the surface to be 'cool', and keep himself 'buttoned up', as he sat with his coat wrapped round him, as though forming a protective skin,[5] but intense emotion was near the surface. In his first contact in therapy, Howard's need for containment of his anxieties is to the forefront.

The container–contained relationship

Bion's ideas about the relationship between the container and contained occupy a very central place in current psychoanalytic thinking. Bion (1962) described a process which begins in early infancy when the infant expels or projects emotions which are too powerful, intense or unknown into the mother.[6] If the mother is receptive to the infant's states of mind, and feels the infant's feelings in herself, it is possible that the infant's states of mind and feelings can be tolerated and known by the mother, and that some sense can then be made of them. Feelings that were too powerful for the infant to hold within her/himself can be thus made tolerable. This, 'contains' the emotions and the mother acts as a 'container' for them. The mother's state of mind in this process of containment, which Bion (1962) called 'reverie', constitute openness to emotional communications of these kinds. That is, the mother's mind does not predetermine the meaning of the infant's communications and needs, but some space is available for uncertainty and ambiguity in communications, and for new ways of thinking about meaning.

Britton (1998) emphasises the aspect of Bion's theory in which the container–contained relationship enables precursors of thought to be transformed from 'nearly sensory-somatic' qualities into 'something more mental'. The nearly sensory-somatic Bion called 'beta-elements', while the something more mental were 'alpha-elements'. The beta-elements, or precursors of thought, leave the mind to enter the realms of somatic, perceptual or action. Britton gives the example of an adult analysand, Miss A, who literally expelled unwanted thoughts down the lavatory. 'There were days when she did this so often that she broke the mechanism' (1998 p. 19). Britton's patient remembered in her adolescence traumatically going to an air raid shelter with her mother and being caught between wishing to escape a suffocating experience in the shelter and her fear of bombs falling in the street:

> Her conflict was intense and apparently unresolvable. She collapsed in the doorway, retaining consciousness but becoming paralysed, mute and entirely without bodily sensations . . . It was this state of anaesthesia that had been used by her internal voice as a threat ever after, compelling her to perform compulsively her irrational activities – 'If you don't do this you will get the feelings.' The feelings she dreaded were actually the experience of having no feelings. (p. 20)

Faced with the predicament of being stuck at the threshold, where both inside and outside felt intolerably dangerous, Miss A sought 'sanctuary and meaning' in her analysis. She tried to find, in other words, a place that was safe and where, once she was inside it, she could gain coherence of her thoughts. Communication takes place through the projection of feelings, unconsciously, as well as through direct verbal communication. It is through the mother/therapist being receptive to the unconscious communications – projections – that the infant/patient has the opportunity of being understood, and of gaining self-understanding and coherence.

If we return now to Howard, there are two points that can be considered about his identity in relation to Miss A's need for containment. Firstly, the experience he described of 'going mad' happened in a way that he did not consciously understand. He did not appear to know which intense emotions drove this behaviour, and when he had such an incident it was experienced as a rupture to his sense of continuity and coherence. His identity was that he was subject to these rupturing passages, and the sense of having a continuous identity was threatened, but restored, through getting to know these processes, in emotional contact with someone else, who performed the function of containing through availability and receptivity. Identity formation occurred within these relationships rather than as a solitary pursuit.

At the beginning of the therapeutic consultation, Howard was unsure whether he would be 'held in mind'. He said he was not a priority. He conveyed in his anxiety that he had to work very hard to contain himself, taking a very tight grip on his piece of paper, wrapping his coat round him and trying to keep emotions in check by playing them down, dismissing them, trying, as it were to make them smaller. This communicated a thought that grown-ups do not need to be looked after in this way, but rather that they aim to do it for themselves; he wants to be a grown-up, and to be seen to be one.

Being held in mind, and not being held in mind

Adolescent anxieties about starting therapy include feeling unsure how it will help, or even will take place. A fragile sense of newly formed and hard-won independence may feel easily crushed. It is important to distinguish between the fragility of adolescent independence and a more deeply seated sense of not being 'held in mind', which has led to patterns of relating to others based on a need for self-sufficiency because there is no expectation of being helped. For Howard, both anxieties about his performance in therapy and a deeper lack of containment were present in varying degrees.

Having a sense of being kept in mind provides the opportunity to reflect on emotional experiences. Having a notion that someone takes in one's thoughts and predicaments and takes them seriously enables communication of inner states to take place.

Case example: Jack

A youth worker was aware that a 17-year-old, Jack, was in difficulties following a traumatic loss. She asked Jack if he would like to talk about himself, but Jack declined, saying talking would only make it worse. The youth worker said OK, but added that it seemed that it must be bad, then. Sometime later she saw Jack was still in the same state of mind and again asked him if he wanted to talk about it. He again declined, but seemed to hesitate as though he would like to talk, if only he could. Some time later, the youth worker met Jack by chance, and this time Jack began the conversation and said that he really would like to talk about it, if possible, because he was very troubled by his thoughts, but he would be nervous about talking to someone.

The youth worker's attention for this young person over a period of time conveyed to Jack that he was kept in mind. Jack had to struggle with the idea he had that talking might increase the difficulty rather than easing it. Britton (1998) describes the experience of an absence of containment as leading to a particular state of mind in which there is reduced hope or faith in the possibility of communicating to others about states of mind:

If a mother fails to absorb the infant's projective identification and resists any attempt by the child to know her mind, she gives the child a picture of a world that does not want to know it and does not want to be known. (1998 p. 23)

He goes on to describe two different relationships based on the failure of the container–contained relationship. The first is akin to the adolescent fear that newly achieved independence will be overtaken and lost in contact with adults. There is a 'fear of being taken in and then destroyed, of one's nature being taken in by another's devouring curiosity and consumed in the process, of oneself being comprehended and nullified during the process' (p. 25). Alternatively, there is a fear that the containing person will deny access, entry and acceptance. These represent a fear of loss of identity and fear of loss of agency.

Containing transition and turbulence in adolescence

Positive experiences of relationships between adolescents and parents involve the capacity to engage, on both sides, in intense negotiations, and the capacity to adapt to the process of adolescence through restructuring relationships (Coleman and Hendry 1999). Thus, at a family level, adolescence is not conflict-free, nor is there absence of potential emotional conflict, but if changes are engaged with and negotiated then the quality of turbulence is transformed.

Containment addresses potential turbulence. Waddell (1998) points out that the re-emergence of conflicts in adolescence 'tests the quality of early containment and internalisation' (p. 128). The adolescent has to make use of the resources that have been provided in infancy and early childhood to understand, make sense of and contain the impact of anxiety, conflict, ambiguity and uncertainty of internal change in adolescence. The adolescent, in other words, draws on the experiences of being contained in infancy and early childhood. Moreover, as well as drawing on past experiences of parenting the adolescent make demands of parents in the present context. These demands may be severe, or intense.

Through the need for containment, the adolescent's quest for identity is undertaken in close relationship with others. If the parent and the adolescent can tolerate experiences of uncertainty, anxiety, change and ambiguity, as well as oscillations of feeling, then the quality of turbulence is transformed. The mental flexibility required by these processes is extremely significant.

If we now return to the case discussed earlier, that of Howard, and consider his adolescence, Howard suggested that the transition through his teens contrasted with the turbulence and dilemmas of the present. Through his teens Howard focused on a structure – study at school and university – and a strategy –

to 'get away from it all'. Now he was uncertain what to do, or what route to take. He had to make decisions. This is like switching from a train journey to a car, to return to Roberts's metaphor. Howard now felt uncertain about the future. His conflicting feelings about his parents, in his current relationships with them, and in his mind, his representations of them, were pushed into the forefront.

It is possible that the smoother transition through his teens had given an illusion of a journey towards adulthood, but that on this journey the problems had been shelved rather than resolved. In trying to 'get away from it all' he had taken flight – understandably, perhaps – from a difficult situation in the family, but he was now left with an unsatisfactory, even dangerous internal situation. In his need to draw on internal resources to make decisions for the future, he had become aware of the difficulty this internal situation presents, and this had made thinking about himself unbearable. As soon as he thought, he drowned those thoughts (literally, given the role of alcohol in his difficulties). In this way he was still 'getting away from it all'.

Between us, Howard and I needed to find a way in which he could use therapy to think his own thoughts and bear the emotional discomfort. But through the lack within of a flexible, containing aspect of himself, the discomfort of his own thoughts was burdensome. He wished to put the burden into me, in the manner of a container–contained relationship. His communication to me was that he wished me to take in these overwhelming thoughts. When I tried to return these in tolerable form, Howard complained that I 'made him think'. He was disturbed by trying to hold his own feelings, and by feelings of depression and loss. Discomfort and depression were the consequences for Howard of engaging with what Anderson and Dartington (1998) call the 'adolescent process':

> If the adolescent is to successfully achieve adulthood, he [sic] must re-negotiate every aspect of his relationship with himself, and with his external and internal objects in a new context – this activity is what we often refer to as the adolescent process. It is like a review of the life that has been lived so far . . . all adolescents have to deal with the experience of being out of balance to some extent. Indeed it seems to be those young people who have the inner strength and resources to bear to continue the experience of being naturally out of balance, as well as an envi-

ronment which can support this, who can achieve the best adjustment in adult life. (1998 p. 3)

There is an echo of Erikson's thinking on the relationship between the individual and society in this formulation of the adolescent process, but with the difference that the emphasis is placed on the process of engagement with relationships, both internal and external. There is an emphasis, in other words, on what happens when the adolescent is in contact with others, and how the processes of containing emotionality leads to the claiming or reclaiming of individuality. The process of seeking identity has to take place through and within relatedness with others.

Summary

- There are diverse approaches to thinking about adolescence, some of which emphasise turbulence and others a smooth transition. There is also a contrast between thinking about adolescence as a difficult but passing phase and seeing long-term psycho-social difficulties located in adolescent turmoil.
- These contradictory views of adolescence are partly resolved by taking a psycho-social approach, in which internal change takes place in contexts which, in conditions of modernity, are uncertain and potentially fragmenting. Transitions are extended and adolescent difficulties may last longer than previously.
- Traditional views of identity, especially Erikson's, tend to underrate the importance of relationships in forming identity. Contemporary thinking about identity emphasises diversity rather than homogeneity.
- The centrality of relationships in forming identity, as distinct from it being a solitary activity, is illustrated through discussion of the container–contained relationship. It is important to distinguish between the adolescent's attempts to sustain her/his own thoughts and a withdrawal from engagement in relationships.

- The availability of containing relationships has a transformational impact on adolescent turbulence. Being kept in mind enables the adolescent to develop and bear the emotional impact of her/his thoughts and feelings. Not being kept in mind leads to exclusion from processes of sharing inner states and to subjecting the adolescent to potential fragmentation, posing threats to the process of identity formation.

BECOMING A SUBJECT IN ADOLESCENCE

This chapter looks closely at what it means to experience being adolescent. It focuses on adolescents' experiences of separation from parental figures and the ways in which they acquire and relate to an emerging adult sexual body, and the qualities of relationships that they form. Recent thinking potentially enriches the way the adolescent process is understood, particularly with regard to the deepening and increasingly complex link between the internal and social worlds. The chapter applies some of these recent ideas, especially those which emphasise the development of subjectivity, to understanding adolescent development. First, there is an exploration, through the discussion of case examples, of ways of thinking about the process of separation from parental figures and the world of childhood. This is followed by a focus on ways in which adolescents experience the impact of bodily changes and their development of attitudes to love and sexuality. Running through both these discussions is an appreciation of how increasing awareness of internal experiences provides a foundation for emerging adolescent subjectivity. This chapter is based on complex theoretical ideas, and the aim is to explain these clearly in conjunction with case examples.

Processes of separating in adolescence

Adolescent subjectivity is developed in a climate of change and transition. Newness and loss pervade these experiences and the adolescent is constantly in a process of evaluating and re-evaluating the meaning of the change or transition. Anxiety and a fluctuating sense of the meaning and implications of experience predominate.

Case example: Hannah

Hannah, now 19, had been in therapy for a year. Her therapy would end when she left for university, in a city in a different part of the country. She was anxious about the ending of her therapy, and about leaving home. She began one session by telling me she had a dream that she had failed her exams. It was just like last year.

She very rarely talked about dreams and was in fact very anxious when unconscious aspects of herself slipped into her sessions. I tried to ask her for some more details about the dream, but she did not want to talk about it and I felt that if I pursued the subject she would close up. She said that her mother had wished her luck with her exams but she knew she did not mean it, because she really did not want her to go to university and leave home. She sounded aggrieved. I said that she had started the session feeling anxious and she seemed to feel she had a lot to handle at the moment, including different ways of looking at how to think about leaving home and therapy.

We did talk then about her dream, in which she spoke again about feeling she was in the same situation as last year, and that after a year's therapy nothing was different. I said it was true that her dream referred to failing exams, and that she felt drawn to similarities with last year, but that it was also possible to think about some differences between then and now. She asked what I meant and I said that she seemed, for example, much more aware of her feelings now, though this awareness put an additional pressure and burden upon her. She was thoughtful for a moment and then said that she did feel she was different and was more aware of her failings. I paused, wondering whether to draw attention to the implicit idea that feelings are synonymous with failings. In fact I said that she did seem to be worried that in the future she would fail in her attempts to manage this burden, of bearing her own feelings herself, after her therapy ended.

There was a pause and she seemed tense. She said she was going to change the subject. She wanted to *know* what would happen in the future. Would she be able to still come to see me? She said she wanted to prepare herself.

This example of Hannah can be discussed through three different aspects of the way she is facing separation from her therapy, and from being a child, living at home to being a student, living away from home. These are separation–individuation, oscillation between different states of mind, or 'positions', and the development of subjectivity, within power relations.

Separation–individuation

Hannah was in a phase of change in which the movement towards greater independence left her feeling anxious, and, in this state, more infantile feelings were pressing upon her. She was in a dilemma about leaving or staying, both wanting to leave and wanting to stay. This relates to the model of separation–individuation which Blos (1962, 1967) applied to adolescence. The adolescent, like the toddler in early childhood, 'hatches' into a separate individual. This explains the contradictory states of mind that can be observed in toddlers, who wish sometimes to be with mother and at others to assert independence and autonomy. Adolescence provides a 'second chance' in development because the eruption of infantile feelings and the developmental importance of regression repeat the 'toddler' dynamics of separation–individuation. Adolescents move out of a childhood immersion in the family, in the same way that toddlers 'hatch' from the symbiotic membrane to become an individual toddler, so that infantile ties to the parents and dependencies on the family are shed. Adolescence is thus marked by both disengagement from the internalised relationships of childhood and engagement – or re-engagement – with infantile wishes, desires and relationships through the impact of the loosening of the relatively predictable world of latency.[1]

Oscillation between different states of mind

Within the therapeutic session, Hannah's anxieties produced two different configurations of relatedness. In the first of these states of mind, she struggled with the impact inside herself about the fears and pains of separating. In this mode, she reported on a dream, which symbolised her experiences, she talked about her anxieties and she located within herself the responsibility for managing her feelings of becoming more separate. She was thoughtful, and she struggled with difficult issues and experiences. In the second mode, when her anxiety about bearing her own feelings became oppressive and overwhelming, she called upon others, who were then invested with responsibilities for the feelings she had about separation. Her emotional experiences became more defined as actions from someone towards her, rather than as emerging from within herself. In this second mode of relating there was a blurring of boundaries between self and others, turbulence and need, together with anxieties which had a more persecutory quality. Thus Hannah was somewhat precariously poised between two ways of relating.

Bion (1963) discussed the way new experiences and the forming of new thoughts about self and others have the effect of making the kind of shift between different ways of relating described in Hannah's case. Bion's thinking developed Klein's views of the paranoid-schizoid and depressive positions,[2] and he supplied the notation PS–D to indicate the two-way nature of this oscillation. Just as being overwhelmed by depressive anxiety, pain, guilt and separateness may trigger a return to PS, so a lessening of persecutory anxiety, an increased awareness of the needs of the other and a greater contact with reality can initiate a move towards D. The oscillation between positions occurs throughout life and is very important in adolescence, because the experiences of newness and change produce this movement between paranoid-schizoid and depressive positions. From an adult point of view, adolescents move between times when they are more negotiable (more D) and times when they are more difficult, demanding, 'unreasonable', etc. (more PS). It is also important to this conceptualisation that the movement is between fields, or states of mind, rather than as progression and regression, or stages of development.

Power, vulnerability and subject relations

A third approach to the material in Hannah's case focuses on the idea that she was involved in an emotional field in which there was a sense of power and vulnerability. This came to the centre of the discussions between us when she became preoccupied with 'knowing', through changing the subject. She introduced her own preoccupation of wanting to know from me about the future, and this had the effect of producing a discontinuity in the session. Her assertion aimed to wrest some power and/or knowledge from me, by challenging me to tell her what would happen, that is, what I had in mind for her, and specifically would I continue to see her. In doing so she found a way, however uncomfortably for both of us, of asserting herself and attending to her needs, so that for a moment the conflict inside her between being independent and being dependent was resolved, as she said, by changing the subject. Thus I had to relate directly to this predicament.

The intersection of issues of achieving greater independence, shifting between different states of mind and power and vulnerability, can be further explored through another case example.

Case example: Lizzie

Lizzie, who was 17 and approaching A levels, complained about being at school. She said she has lost all interest in studying and couldn't wait to leave. She said she was bored, and wanted to work and earn money. She experienced her peers as immature and said she was much happier in the company of older people. She spent much of her time in therapy talking about boyfriends, who were always much older than she was. She said she expected older boyfriends to be able to look after her better than boyfriends of her own age. In these relationships an initial enthusiasm with extravagant hopes was quickly turned to bitter disappointment and disillusionment, when she felt her boyfriend had let her down. Unperturbed, and defiant, she continued to search for another, who would not disappoint her.

Lizzie seemed caught up in a repetitive pattern in her relationships, in which her boredom with school and her own age peers, together with seeking a solution through acquiring an older boyfriend, indicated a difficulty she had in her development. There was a paradoxical wish for independence and being looked after in a childlike way. There was, it seems, conflict and anxiety around independence and separateness. Her repeated pattern of relationships showed her both clinging to childhood wishes to be looked after by a parent figure, and defending herself against feeling separate. Her relationships repeated Oedipal[3] conflicts and desire. Whenever Lizzie became more aware of the intensity of her wish to avoid feeling separate and alone, she became intensely anxious and then she clings more tenaciously to her defensive and repetitive patterns. In effect she turned to a more paranoid-schizoid way of relating, in which an idealised relationship was felt to solve her problems and obviate the need to develop a sense of separateness within herself.

In this predicament she was driven to achieve a powerful position, with regard to the difficulties she felt she faced in her internal world and her intersubjective relations, and thus to avoid the intense feelings of vulnerability she would feel through ordinary dependency on others. But because she was unaware (and terrified) of the unconscious processes that drove her, she was intensely subject to these forces, rather than being able to modify their intensity through reflection.

Kennedy (1998) makes a useful distinction between being 'subject to' and 'subject of' the forces and experiences with which the individual is in contact, from both within and without. Being 'subject to' acknowledges the process of being on the receiving end of internal and external forces, with a consequent limitation of agency. Being 'subject of' implies the capacity to appropriate the forces acting on and in the subject – to state for oneself. The movement from being 'subject to' to being 'subject of' is undertaken through an inward reflective process, which takes account of and appropriates the experience.

Becoming a subject in adolescence is linked closely with experiences of separation and, through reflection on experience, being able to take into account aspects of oneself and one's situation in the social world. Cahn (1998) has begun to apply these ideas to adolescence. He has conceptualised adolescence as being concerned primarily with 'subjectivation' (becoming a subject). This is taken to mean the process where the adolescent confers meaning to intrapsychic and intersubjective experiences of change. Thus the adolescent develops characteristic ways of relating to new experiences, primarily in relationships. There may be adolescents who tend to relate newness back to the familiar or already known, while others are open to the unknown. Preference for the familiar and known leads to repetitive or mechanical ways of relating, while at the other extreme a privileging of newness over the familiar can lead to a manic search for excitement. Between these two extremes are oscillating moments of openness and closure. Subjectivity is not 'hatched' (as Blos described), but it – rather elusively – comes into focus and then recedes; or it focuses on one aspect before another takes precedence. Kennedy (2000) argues that the sense of becoming a subject is experienced around times of opening up and closing down, of being present and absent, and appearing and disappearing. Adolescents are thus involved in an uncertain and essentially anxious process, of discovering moments of 'being themselves', in the course of developing their sense of their own subjectivity. When they are, or feel themselves to be, 'subject to' experiences from within or outside, that is, from the social world, there results a sense of inauthenticity and frustration.

Case example: Joseph

Joseph was agonised by his relationships with his peers in a sixth-form college. He felt he was rather stuck in a role he took up, as being at the centre of decision-making in his group. He found that if he felt he wished to relate to others in a less powerful way he was not listened to or taken seriously. As a consequence he began to feel very frustrated with his peers, and misunderstood by them.

Joseph did not talk much about his home life to his friends. He tried to protect himself from having to discuss a background he found alternatively painful and humiliating. His father was frequently depressed, and Joseph was very intolerant of his depression. He complained with intense frustration that his father did not do anything to help himself. Thus he could not bear his father's states of mind, which probably were in fact quite provocative.

Joseph was initially quite unaware that he could not tolerate depression or depressive feelings in himself, and that his father mirrored for him his own difficulty in tolerating depressed feelings and vulnerability. Whenever he was involved in the kind of relating in which depressive feelings emerged, he withdrew from the relationship, with a critical thought that he and others ought to 'pull themselves together'. In his therapy, he began to become aware of and tolerate his depressed feelings and vulnerability. This led him to feel more sympathetic to his father and to also engage with his peers in discussions of an emotional nature. He could, for example, let them comment on his emotional states without feeling attacked.

Joseph's situation illustrates how reflection upon and containment of unbearable aspects of the self increase the possibilities of separating from parental figures and generating greater internal independence. Joseph was 'subject to' being like his father internally, and his fear of depressed feelings led him to compensate through taking up powerful roles with his friends. Through reflection in his therapy he was able to get to know these aspects of himself and gradually to feel less terrorised by them. This introduced a more depressive field in which toleration of his own feelings was accompanied by greater sympathy for his father and greater flexibility in his relationships with his peers.

Then, instead of having to adopt powerful, knowing positions with them, he was more able to enter the to-and-fro of discussion about himself and others, and he could be more open about himself, his emotional life and his background, selectively, with others. Powerfulness based on avoidance and denial of vulnerability was transformed into power/knowledge based on reflection on inner states, leading to more flexibility in his subject positions. He did not have to be the powerful leader all the time. He thus became more 'subject of' than 'subject to', and an identity based on but separate from his childhood began to emerge.

The perspective of subject relations is recent and it has not been applied extensively to adolescence, nor is there a coherently developed infantile model of subject relations to which professionals working with adolescents can refer. One account is provided by Urwin (1998). She discusses how an infant's subjectivity is located in 'social practices which occur frequently and regularly in particular infants' lives, such as feeding, bathing and other care taking operations, greetings and farewells, certain forms of regularised play and games and so on' (p. 282). The prioritising of social practices cuts across the individual–context dichotomy, and raises the question as to where individuals are 'positioned' in a particular discourse. Second, Urwin creates a central place in her thinking for the ubiquity of power relations, which, following Foucault, she claims 'are integral to the production and reproduction of discourses' (p. 284). Power is relative and depends on positioning within discourses, so that individuals are not statically once and for all powerful or powerless. Power relations 'interpenetrate the reproduction of subjectivity throughout children's development' (p. 285). Urwin claims that these developments do not in any way replace the emphasis on emotionality and unconscious processes that are central to psychoanalytic thinking, but rather provide a framework for thinking about another domain – subjectivity – within a psychoanalytic discourse.[4]

Urwin applies this model to infant development. The one-year-old, in his glorious and majestic omnipotence, entertains an illusion of control while also becoming increasingly aware of dependency on adults. Adults can intervene to reposition the baby in more 'adult' directions, while the baby's discovery of separation is experienced as annihilating. A new relation between baby and mother emerges, in which the assertion of more adult and powerful positioning is brought about through the suppression of more dependent positions. The tension between two conflicting wishes – to be independent and to be dependent – leads to the infant oscillating between the two, so that gaining one implies a loss of the other.

In my own experience I recall observing an infant, Samantha, who at 17 months 13 days was

> playing with some shoes. She selected a pair of her mother's and put one foot into one of these shoes, looking serious, concentrating. She stopped, took her foot out, and ran down the corridor. She ran back with a packet of baby wipes, calling out 'mummy'. (Briggs 1997)

Samantha tried out, quite literally, what it felt like to be in mummy's shoes, but a baby self who needed a mummy reasserted itself, and she urgently aimed to put mother in role, and herself in a dependent baby position rather than a grown-up mummy role. She oscillated between taking a powerful position but abandoned this when her need for a mother became predominant. It can be inferred that anxiety – a fear of loss of mother and her position of being mothered – lay in her movement from one position to another.

Adolescents, in this model, position themselves more or less powerfully, depending on the way vulnerabilities are felt within the self. Those adolescents – like Lizzie and Joseph – who become stuck in a kind of powerful position betray difficulties in relationship to dependency, vulnerability and loss internally. Joseph's development was freed up when he could tolerate his own vulnerability, and he could then move between different subject positions, intrapsychically and intersubjectively. Hannah experienced a moment, when she demanded knowledge from me, when she was engaged in the conflict between power and vulnerability. Assertiveness took place in a context in which she was aware of her fragility. Urwin concludes that 'we are produced as capable of assertive action, yet also fragile and acutely vulnerable' (p. 321). Lizzie showed that fear of vulnerability and the search for relatively powerful positions can lead to repetitious and conservative behaviour in the face of anxiety.

Relating to the body: puberty and the emergence of adult love and sexuality

Central to becoming a subject in adolescence is the assimilation or appropriation of the images of and relationships to the bodily changes of puberty. Internal conflict stems from the way this process of ownership is accomplished, and the difficulties that are encountered. Laufer and Laufer (1984) discuss the way that conflict revolves around the 'ownership of the body' (p. 38): 'One important issue is whether the adolescent can emotionally experience his [sic] mature body as belonging to himself or reacts as if his body still belonged to his mother, who first cared for it' (p. 39). There are many traditional and recent views about the appropriation by the adolescent of her/his maturing body, and the consequent emergence of sexual and loving subjectivity. Here three of these 'routes' will be explored: appropriating the power of infantile phantasy, taking an aesthetic route and entering into sexual discourses.

Appropriating the power of infantile phantasy

In the classical view, puberty springs upon the adolescent, from the quiescence of latency, breaking down 'an internal system of civilisation; a structure of defences whereby law and order and sublimations have been established to some extent' (Hoxter 1964 p. 14). This leads to an awareness of power, either as an intense process to which one is subject, or as an infiltration of powerfulness into the subject, so that there is an awareness that physical and mental power can be used. Thus the adolescent has the physical means to put infantile phantasies into practice. 'He [*sic*] can really attack, destroy, rob, murder or commit suicide, and he can really have sexual experiences of a heterosexual or homosexual kind' (Hoxter 1964 p. 13).

Recapitulation of the Oedipal conflicts of early childhood has long been considered an essential aspect of the turbulence of adolescence, for boys and girls (Jones 1922, Waddell 1998). The intense anxieties produced by the intense desires breaking through and breaching the defences of latency lead to a wish either to deny sexuality or to act.

The process of accepting the bodily changes may become fraught. The adolescent oscillates between states of mind in which s/he more wishes to be – or identify with – being a child to his/her parents, and times when s/he wishes to move forward to being *like* the parents. To progress requires forgiveness for past hurts, such as being excluded from the parental relationship and indeed for the range of humiliations, pains and narcissistic wounds experienced in childhood. This involves allowing for not having a perfect childhood or even the childhood that one wished to have.

Taking the aesthetic route

The vividness of the aesthetic encounter in adolescence may be profound, almost as Sacks (1986) describes the impact of a heightened sense of smell in transforming everyday experiences. Rose Tremain (1998) in *The Way I Found Her* begins her story and her character's first awareness of puberty with an aesthetic encounter:

> I once thought beauty was something found only in old paintings. It never really occurred to me that ordinary people could be beautiful, here and now. And then I saw – that day in July – that they could be and that my mother was one of them.

This awakening with its new view of the world will have implications that will be worked out and worked through in the course of the story. It is arresting that this narrative – albeit fictional – shows adolescence emerging through an encounter with beauty.[5] Perhaps this avoids in a quasi-intellectual way the problem of aggression and sexuality. The aesthetic encounter is a way of awakening to adult sexuality, and the potential for adult love.

Case example: Stan

A young man I saw for a therapeutic consultation, Stan, told me he did not get on with his girlfriend; they argued and they seemed not to have similar interests. He then looked at me directly and said 'I do love her though', as though to make a clear point; that it was not his girlfriend that was the problem, in his perspective, but rather his problem in loving.

Anna Dartington used to ask adolescents as they talked about their entangled and troublesome relationships 'but do you love him/her?', and I think thus acknowledged for the adolescent that an adult was prepared to take their loves seriously. Using Urwin's model of emergent power relations, it could be said that this is a way of promoting a more powerful, adult position in the adolescent. On the other hand, taking the adolescent's wish to love seriously involves acknowledging both the complexity of the emotion, the oscillations between love and hate, and the potential violence in the adolescent's awakening to this quality of experience. Lewis Little, the hero of Tremain's novel became entangled in a state of murderousness and guilt:

In the night, after beginning to read *Crime and Punishment* I had a dream about Raskolnikov and I woke up sweating. I didn't know whether, in the nightmare, I'd been Raskolnikov or his intended victim, Alena Ivanovna. For a moment it seemed to me as if everything in my attic room was yellow and I felt suffocated and sick. (p. 110)

These nightmares and the confusion of roles – murderer or victim – appear as the flipside of the aesthetic conflict. The emphasis here is on the disturbing impact of new emotional experiences, and with Bion's idea of 'catastrophic change'. This term refers to the view that 'all development brings in its train the threat of catastrophe to the mind' (Hinshelwood 1989), which is ultimately its annihilation or breakdown. The violence of the explosiveness of catastrophic change proposes that the aesthetic conflict is being subject to the impact of violence within, which degrades the 'beautiful' object.

For Bion, catastrophic change occurred in the little oscilla- tions between the paranoid schizoid and the depressive positions. A movement towards loving involves anxieties and pains about the other person, and being separate. When concern and guilt feel intolerable, the anxiety about annihilation in the paranoid schizoid position is re-experienced. It is impossible, Bion wrote, to 'escape the odium inseparable from the mind. Refuge is sure to be sought in mindlessness, sexualisation, acting-out, and degrees of stupor' (Bion 1970 p. 126). Perhaps stupor refers to the adolescent's propensity to sleep in! The 'odium' of the mind, or a similar notion, 'abjection', that Kristeva (1982) refers to is located very close to the body, and to love.

The idea of catastrophic change at puberty was expressed succinctly by a 13-year-old boy, who said that though he was growing it was not a problem for him, but he had two friends who did have problems, because for one of them his bones were growing faster than his muscles and ligaments, and with the other friend it was the other way round; his muscles were growing faster than his bones. One of them was very stiff and the other was very floppy. This disaster also indicated that two qualities that had been in synchrony with each other until puberty were now violently opposed to each other, an acute problem for the container–contained relationship.

Engaging with sexual discourses

Traditionally, thinking about adolescence has emphasised the development, through puberty, of adult sexuality and its impact on the individual. This does not take into account the multiplicities and diversities which prevail in contemporary contexts, and the complex ways in which adolescents have to engage with current themes, or discourses, about sexuality. A discourse, as Foucault discussed the term, refers to 'the way in which meanings cohere around an assumed central proposition, which gives them their value and significance' (Hollway 2000 p. 14).[6] Foucault pointed out that sex had been 'put into discourses' which regulated the development of the individual, and the species:

> [sex] was at the pivot of two axes which developed the entire political technology of life. On the one hand it was tied to the discipline of the body; the harnessing, intensification and distribution of forces, the adjustment and economy of energies. On the other hand it was applied to the regulation of populations . . . sex was the means of access both to the life of the body and the life of the species. (1979, p. 145)

Though seemingly at odds with psychoanalytic accounts of sexuality, Foucault's work in fact contextualises and provides an underpinning philosophical standpoint for contemporary thinking.[7] Foucault provides a way of thinking about different discourses of sexuality, and his conceptualisations take into account the multiplicity of contemporary sexual discourses. Contemporary discourses include the 'promiscuous discourse', which holds that 'sex with many partners can be both pleasurable and harmless' (Hollway 1989), alongside a discourse, post AIDS, of the fear of the damaging effects of sex, especially male homosexual sex. There is a discourse about 'heterosexual erotic love', which is a specific cultural product (Chodorow 1995, p. 91). Dominant 'discourses' can exclude those of other cultures, and, though gay sexuality has increased its status, becoming more visible and tolerated in some sections of society, this is still a 'deeply stigmatised identity' (Edwards 1997).

Sexual discourses are diverse, and they are also ubiquitous. For adolescents the ubiquity of discourses of sex mean that it 'penetrates and controls everyday pleasure', it 'incites and intensifies' and is 'produced' by talk (including media talk and images) about sexuality (Foucault 1979). It is indeed extremely difficult for adolescents to turn away from such dominance, and to still find an identity. Being a 'nerd' may be an oppositional and derogated alternative 'discourse' for a contemporary adolescent, but it contests or resists the mainstream of pervasive sexuality, rather than arising in isolation to it.

Since sexual discourses are all-pervasive, the body becomes

the focus – or 'site' – for the experiencing of self and society, and a preoccupation with issues of control, integrity and autonomy. The body is suffused with potential meaning through intersubjective experiences. Just making contact with others has this effect. Additionally, developing an identity is inevitably connected with developing a bodily identity, and subjectivity must be thought of as emerging from a mind/body unity, rather than from a split between the two. Bodily and emotional unity may be demonstrated through the embodiment of emotionality. For example, words we use – being 'affected', 'upset', 'touched', 'moved', 'shocked', 'alarmed', etc. – indicate this unity and embodiment of experience.[8] Mental processes can symbolise these embodied experiences.

The working upon bodily experience, transforming it or symbolising it, connects with both an old tradition in psychoanalysis, which was central to Freud's early work, and a current psycho-social viewpoint. The body is a 'theatre' (McDougall 1986) and states of body – for example, being held – can be transferred through symbolism, dreaming and phantasising, into states of mind. This has a particular relevance for thinking about eating disorders (see Chapter 7). Bion's development of the mind on the model of the digestive system makes parallel physical and mental states. 'It is important', he wrote, when discussing the transformation of 'beta elements' into 'alpha', 'to distinguish between memories and undigested facts'. Alpha function in this analogy is the stomach, the storehouse, in which experiences are transformed into thoughts, memories and symbolic representation. 'Beta elements are stored but differ from alpha elements in that they are not so much memories as undigested facts' (Bion 1962 pp. 6–7). Bion's model of the mind can be applied to the continual transformation of self in situated contexts, when the raw experience of self are subject to processes of reflection.

Through engagement in socio-cultural and interpersonal contact, the body is in constant transformation through experience, so that there is 'a continuous stream of affect between the everyday social environment and the ways in which people might come to subjectively experience their bodies to feel who they are' (Buytendijk 1974, p. 174).

Adolescents are particularly affected by these processes. The experience of puberty has a tremendous and turbulent impact in social situations, demonstrating tension between the containment of bodily experience, through reflection, attempting to control turbulence,[9] and managing what is happening internally, the fluidity of experiences.[10] Recently, attention to the experiences of adolescents, especially girls, shows the interaction of internal and social factors.

Menstruation has been a focus for these discussions. Prendergast (1995) suggests that 'experiences of bodily shock, fragmentation and disorder accompany menstrual experience in the West' (p. 210). The 'body is in the mind', in a preoccupying sense, so that the adolescent is constantly involved in managing, controlling or containing experiences. In some circumstances, the adolescent defensively distances from bodily experiences and objectifies the body, or else dissociates from it. Awareness of emerging adult embodiment is developed as much through social relations – especially school peers – and through the containing capacity of the mother, as through 'identification' with parents. Sayers's (1991) reports of accounts of girls reaching puberty show mothers to be either dismissing of the girl's emotional experience (that is how it is remembered) or objectifying of 'it' in the way they discuss menstruation and sexuality. Thus it is the context in which emerging adult sexuality is contained which is the most powerful factor in adolescent engagement with sexual discourses.

Case example: Satya

Satya began therapy when she was 18, worried about her development. An aspect of her experience of puberty was illustrated by a dream. She was in a lift in which she regularly travelled. On this occasion it travelled as usual, floor by floor, until it reached the 12th. Then it took off, exploding upwards and she was fearful both that it would not stop and that it would crash to earth. The understanding we came to share about this dream was that each floor represented a year of her life; the 12th floor related to the onset of puberty, which began when she was 11. After puberty, the gradual progress, floor by floor, or year by year, was replaced with a violent explosiveness. Satya's experience of the transition from childhood to adolescence was then explosive, fearful and catastrophic.

The impact of puberty and early adolescence was complicated by Satya's sexual experiences at this time. Her guilt about her rather precocious sexuality turned into an attempt to make sure others did not notice and she assumed a rather excessively childlike appearance. In her looks and in her clothes, she seemed more like a young girl than a young woman. She portrayed the adult world as monstrous, and she talked about not being able to find a path to join the worlds in which adults lived. She knew she had to go into the adult world, but she was terrified of it. She wanted to have a boyfriend but she was terrified of closeness. She had a sense of not being integrated in her body, which was represented in dreams of houses which had 'bits' stuck on randomly, and haphazardly, rather than in a planned or integrated development. She felt herself to be missing an important part of herself, which she thought of as bodily, and which felt dirty and ugly, but which she could not describe in words.[11]

For Satya adult sexual bodies had become abject and contaminated. Kristeva (1982) in developing the idea of abjection, controversially perhaps, represented female sexuality as an uncontainable flow, as characterised by menstrual blood. The abject includes food and bodily incorporation, abjection towards bodily waste, the horror of the corpse and towards sexual difference. As a descriptive category, the abject does capture something of the awfulness and degradation of the way some adolescents experience the body. In groups, the most debased, despised feelings and thoughts can be projected into others, and this makes life especially miserable when the others in the group return these feelings, and others, in taunts or verbal and physical assaults.[11]

As well as recapitulating early infantile and Oedipal development, for girls the experience of puberty 'introduces its own fundamental changes and challenges to physical and psychological integrity' (Plaut and Hutchinson 1986 p. 418). These authors view male and female experiences of puberty as qualitatively different, there being for the girl especially a fundamental or new experience to account for at puberty. The impact of puberty then needs to be taken seriously as a transforming experience, and as having meaning in its own right. This leads to the view that much is to be discovered about 'how romantic and sexual desires are formed during adolescence, when there is a coming together of childhood, culture and pubertal development, and that as we come to know more, we will find that this period is especially crucial' (Chodorow 1995 p. 102).

Emergent masculinity

Male experiences of puberty may also be experienced as diverse. In general terms it has been suggested that while young women seem to maintain relatedness with others – even if disappointed in the quality of the relationships – young men find it difficult to maintain this kind of contact, and become divided internally (Sayers 1991).

Case example: Jerry

> One boy, Jerry, 11, experienced puberty as exciting and dangerous. His discussions were interspersed with talk of power kites that 'go high' and of having a 'six-inch knife'. He was preoccupied with size and power and risk. He told me his kite might not be the biggest one but it still might pull him off the ground.

Jerry had difficulty in maintaining contact in relationships, and the manic excitement and violence of his feelings at puberty threatened to split him off further from others and thus from the possibility of having these feelings modulated through containment. The vicissitudes of bodily experiences at puberty can lead to abject experiences.

Case example: Harry

> Harry, 17, told me that his life had changed twice in adolescence. He portrayed himself as having a rather miserable childhood. He started his therapy as a rather insubstantial figure, wrapped usually in a bulky jacket and baseball cap. He spoke in a low monotone and complained of sleeplessness and depression.
>
> Interactions at home were very thinly described and he could not with any substance talk about the kind of child he had been. He was not really able to describe satisfying times with his parents, or convey a sense of being able to call on them when he was in difficulties. This rather abject picture of himself was redeemed when he found, quite by chance when he was 12, a sudden and surprising ability to play golf. Indeed he was so good that he obtained sponsorship at a national level. When he was 15 he found, almost as suddenly, that his skills stopped developing. He lost his sponsorship and his hopes of being a sports star.

After the loss of his hopes of sporting stardom, Harry could not find new routes to satisfaction within himself. He seemed to have few resources inside himself to draw on and mourn his loss.

It seemed important that the discovery of the sporting ability arose out of a childhood which seemed not to be nourishing. Harry's hope of becoming a sporting star is a common fantasy in adolescence, made all the more poignant and tantalising by the fact that it nearly became attainable – he found a talent in himself and got within touching distance of it. The loss of his sporting aspirations was painful and difficult to mourn. On the other hand, his suddenly acquired sporting ability had the effect of lifting him above the misery of his internal world, and the limitations of his relationships. Sayers (1991) illustrates the way adolescents idolise others, mainly male sporting or music stars. Blos (1984) approved hero worship and idolisation, and the cult of poster personality, which adorns teenage bedrooms. Sayers (1991 p. 117), with a wealth of self-reports, show that the heroes and idols of adolescence are long remembered. Harry, though, was taking himself as hero. His sudden emergence of a physical prowess following puberty brought a sense of power and achievement, triumphing briefly over his miserable childhood. The hope for sporting success was harnessed as a means of saving himself from his inner world. It was stuck onto his identity like Satya stuck adulthood on to her body. Harry wished to turn himself into an idol and in losing this possibility lost his 'ideal'. Hanna Segal (1995) considers the difference between idealisation and ideal:

> Idealisation is a distortion of realities and a dangerous stance, since it is invariably accompanied by splitting and projection – idealising oneself and one's ideas or groups at the expense of paranoid attitudes to others. Having ideals is very different; it is not pathological to hope for a better future; for instance for peace and to strive for it, while recognising how hard it is to attain, and that the opposition to it comes not only from others but also has its roots in ourselves. (1995 p. 204)

Summary

- This chapter has explored the meaning of subjectivity in adolescence, the process in which adolescents have diverse experiences of bodily changes and separation from familiar ways of relating as a child.

- While traditional views of separating are unidirectional, recent thinking suggests that the conceptualisation of movements between positions provides a more flexible and adaptable way of looking at adolescent development. The movement between paranoid-schizoid and depressive positions, and the taking up of subject positions within different contexts of power and vulnerability, are two ways in which understanding of adolescent development is deepened.
- Adolescents may experience both powerful and vulnerable aspects of themselves. The case examples show adolescents struggling within these dimensions to make sense of change, separating and their relationships with others. Change is experienced in complex ways, and has deep emotional impact.
- A very important consideration in adolescent development is the embodiment of change. The changes of puberty and the engagement with having a mature body lead to engagement with adult sexuality and love. Adolescents take diverse 'routes' to establishing gendered identity, including appropriating the power of infantile phantasies, encountering the aesthetic, and entering into sexual discourses.
- Adolescent development needs to be considered as taking place through the interplay of internal and social processes. Childhood, pubertal development and culture interact to create different meanings for male and female adolescents in the appropriation of maturity.

3

ETHNICITY AND IDENTITY IN ADOLESCENCE

One of the important ways in which a unitary sense of identity formation in adolescence has been severely disturbed is through the impact of the diversity of ethnic identities. This chapter explores the impact of ethnicities on identity construction in adolescence, through developing and applying the discussion of subjectivity and identity in Chapter 2. How these considerations affect thinking about therapeutic work is discussed, and illustrated with case examples.

Across cultural boundaries

Ethnic identity formation in adolescence involves both social and internal processes: 'the point of confluence of economic, political, cultural and psychic processes . . . where multiple subject positions are juxtaposed, contested, proclaimed or disavowed' (Brah 1996, p. 208). Thus it is important, following the discussion in Chapter 2, to consider the specific meanings of 'becoming a subject' (subjectivation) that emerge for adolescents in cross-cultural, multicultural and different cultural contexts.

Cahn's view of subjectivation is that the individual adolescent is involved in an internal struggle and a social process in becoming a subject, leading to a sense of self in the world (individual identity) and holding a sense of truth(s). Alternatively, the process may be unfulfilling, and may 'lure him/her into a closed ideology or delusion, alienating or imprisoning him/her and distorting his/her world' (Cahn 1998, p. 159). Involvement in the struggle to find and establish identity in terms of ethnicity involves the adolescent, especially the minority ethnic adolescent, in difficult and exacting processes of developing cohesiveness, a sense of self, within complex and divisive contexts. How socio-cultural practices become produced and reproduced as individual development and identity is central to understanding these processes. Professionals working with adolescents from a range of cultures have to be sensitive to and understanding of different nuances of meaning, and multiple, plural contexts. This has been shown to be important in therapeutic work, though this kind of work still requires much more detailed exploration (Bains 2001).

Case example: Pavan

Pavan, an Indian woman of 18, told me on her first meeting with me, that she had asked to come to the clinic because she had heard it was a 'good place'. She came, she said, from an extended family in which her grandparents and her father's sister and her family lived in the same household as her parents and siblings.

Pavan said she was doing A levels, and she was worried about them, as she had no confidence in her work and she needed her A levels to be able to leave home. In fact her work had been going downhill for some time. She said she was very anxious about her school work, and felt urgently that some help was needed. In a despondent, pessimistic way she asked me how long she would have to come to therapy for it to make a difference. She thought it would take years for her therapy to help her, and she did not have that long – her A-levels were in a matter of months. When I asked her about cultural issues, in the context of her starting therapy, she very definitely said no, cultural issues were not important to her, and added that 'all my friends are white'.

Pavan's response to the question of culture created ambiguity. She seemed to convey that she was quite comfortable in white company, and it may be thought of as a way of reassuring me, a white man, that she had no problem with me. On the other hand, if taken literally, it may have meant there were problems with same-culture friends. Talking about culture directly seemed to make her anxious, an important consideration at the beginning of a therapeutic relationship when the adolescent may already feel anxious and vulnerable. The adolescent may respond in

49

a compliant way to thinking directly about this issue, and the topic may have been raised many times at school and in other contexts. Pavan did seem to be quite protective of me from the beginning. She was very descriptive about her family structure, and explained it to me to put me in the picture. Perhaps she expected me to misunderstand her situation; perhaps she thought the only model of a family in my mind was of a nuclear family. At the same time as being descriptive, she denied the close family connections a name – she did not assert, for example, that she lived in an Indian family. As the discussion continued, the wish to leave home and to get away from her culture appeared to be very linked. The discussion of leaving home suggested a cultural issue was important, since this is not usually an uncontested option for a young woman in an Indian family.

There are pressures on ethnic-minority adolescents to assimilate to another culture. The experience of starting therapy is a cross-cultural experience for a young woman like Pavan, and her initial contact with me constituted an accommodation to other cultures, the culture of psychotherapy, and the culture of the clinic. Often, 'psychotherapy is perceived as a type of treatment that has its roots firmly planted in the host culture' (Bains 2001, p. 68). Pavan's accommodation was accompanied by her awareness of a problem in herself and within her family, which had led to her starting therapy. She may have had a very wide range of feelings and thoughts about this, and like many adolescents who refer themselves, may have started therapy with a doubtful or ambiguous relationship with her family in mind. The quality of Pavan's early communications, that is, the way she talked about her family, suggested that a boundary (between siblings and cousins) was blurred. She seemed to be under an imperative to get away from home, and given this she appeared to be reassuring herself that she had found a 'good place', which would help. She was thus in a vulnerable position between two cultures in which communications are tinged with ambiguity and multiple meanings.

Two possibilities thus emerged very early in this therapy; first, that Pavan had an anxious approach to meeting a white man in the role of therapist in a new culture, and, expecting not to be understood, was fearful and thus tried to reassure and protect. The second possibility was that there is a problem within her family, which she needed to get away from, and that this seemed to mean making a move across cultures, away from her own and potentially rejecting it. Rejection of her family and culture, together with an idealisation of English culture and the 'good' place of the clinic, may also be Pavan's attempts to deal with her difficulties, and these too place her in a vulnerable position. Thus in terms of her identity, Pavan was developing within a context in which the potential loss of her identity as an Indian woman was accompanied by anxiety about acceptance across a cultural boundary. Like many young people from ethnic minority backgrounds, she started therapy when there was 'a deepening and widening divide between themselves and family members, mainly parents' (Bains 2001, p. 66).

Tolerating and not tolerating difference

Identity is constructed around issues of sameness and difference, within power relations. 'Every identity is founded on an exclusion and, in that sense, is an "effect of power". There must be something which is external to an identity' (Hall 2000, p. 234). Ethnic identity is formed in a context of racism, so that the experience of negative experiences in social contact has a dynamic effect on the process of assimilation and acculturation, which are internalised. Racism is, of course, a powerfully destructive experience, which is extremely hurtful to victims, and also denies their status as individuals, as subjects. It occurs in a paranoid-schizoid field, in which unwanted or unbearable aspects of the self are split off and put into others (Rustin 1991) in order to avoid an experience of difference, and to sustain a distorted sense of superior power. Racism in these terms lies deeply configured in the unconscious, and racist dynamics are extremely early, primitive and infantile. For example, Tan (1993) points out that extreme violence and hatred are central to racism, and that they are used to aim to obliterate difference. He adds that 'difference serves as a constant reminder of the painful early experience of impending loss of the "good breast" which for some infants is unbearable' (p. 33).

The racist subject aims to construct a divided world, in which sameness and difference are equated with goodness and badness, and in which the 'bad' is located outside, as an enemy or demonised other.

The idea that unbearable or intolerable experiences of separation are a motive force in racism connects with the adolescent preoccupation with separation from internal parental figures. The process of forming identity, of sorting the 'me' from the 'not me' and differentiating, therefore, sameness and difference, are to the forefront of adolescent experiences. Tolerating difference, and thus moving from a paranoid-schizoid into a depressive field, occurs in the process of flux, in which the adolescent characteristically develops. In adolescence, attempts to be open to difference, and moments of closure, can follow each other quite rapidly, movement in one direction or another being triggered by what might seem to be a small event.

Back (1997) provides an example in which friendships between two white British and a Vietnamese young man briefly flourished, and then broke down under the impact of difference being too difficult to tolerate. The painfulness that results was substantial. When the Vietnamese man was asked by a new youth club worker how to spell his name – Tanyi – one of the white friends, Cliff, answered 'just write it Tony'. Back points out that Anglicisation of names was accommodated by the Vietnamese youth on the grounds that the whites could not pronounce their names properly. But on this occasion, and within the rather precarious nature of their friendship, Cliff exerted dominance, and his resentment of difference was communicated. Tanyi stopped seeing the other boys and stopped going to the youth club. Though white young men justified the absence of Vietnamese young men from the youth club with the view that 'they just like to keep themselves to themselves', Tanyi told a youth worker that he had stopped attending because of the racist 'verbals' he suffered, and that he did not 'want them to use me as something to play with'. Thus Tanyi expressed the impact of the projective processes to which he was subjected, that he was scapegoated within this group, and that he was objectified as a 'toy'. Within the power relationship between Cliff and Tanyi, negative experiences of cross-cultural contact are projected into Tanyi, who withdraws into a same-cultural network.

This example shows the potential fluidity of group formation and its precariousness. It also illustrates in microcosm how contact across cultures can tenuously be made, and then the power with which the negative attributions and the powerful assertions of sameness – on the basis of agreeing with the dominant – lead to withdrawal. The more threatened an individual, family and culture feel, the more the withdrawal leads to organisation based on sameness. This has a protective function for the oppressed individual, family and culture, but it also occurs in a persecutory field in which negative experiences are taken in, or internalised, to become part of identity (Bains 2001).

If we return to Pavan's case, the complexities of negative experiences, in the context of making contact with a new, different culture, and with a white therapist are evident. The sense of badness within, and her protective approach to me, may indicate a problem within her family, a way of dealing with anticipated experiences of not being understood, and an expectation of negative experience:

> The overarching context is not simply multicultural, but one which contains cultural hierarchies, dominant ideologies as well as cultural and political struggle. The individual's psyche cannot escape these issues, it reflects them and is obliged to constantly find ways to resolve and survive them. (Lowe 2001)

In the therapeutic encounter, it is extremely difficult to be clear in which domain the meaning of experiences such as these belong. Bains emphasises that

> It should be noted that when dealing with the psychological effects of social processes (i.e. racism) it is extremely difficult to differentiate between whether a defence is dysfunctional (e.g. a result of underlying conflicts) or functional (e.g. appropriate) or both. However, perceived experiences of racism do require the attention from the therapist and appropriate intervention when necessary to engage the young person in the therapeutic process. (Bains 2001, p. 68)

Cultural identity and hybridity

Adolescents seeking therapy are often involved in a 'deepening and wider divide between themselves and family members, mainly parents' (Bains 2001, p. 66). Thus therapists and other professional workers become involved in complex patterns of individual and cultural change, and an encounter, in 'juxtaposed, contested, proclaimed or disavowed' dimensions, with the meaning of 'multicultural' or cross-cultural connections and change.

Thus therapists and other professionals are working now from positions in which everyone – professionals, institutions, adolescents, their families and networks – is involved in pluralistic cultural contexts. In the background is the contradictory, even paradoxical experience of 'globalisation', which makes everything the same, and, pulling in the opposite direction, increases diversity, so that there is no longer a monolithic, binary difference absolute sameness and absolute difference, but

> every concept or meaning is inscribed in a chain or in a system within which it refers to the other, to other concepts (meanings) by means of the systematic play of differences . . . meaning here has no origin or final destination, cannot be finally fixed, is always in process, 'positional' along a spectrum. (Hall 2000, p. 216)

The contradictory presence of increasing sameness and new forms of difference is most vividly seen in the problems and possibilities of multiculturalism. Hall makes this contradictory state of multiculturalism clear. On the one hand there are transitional elements which appear to open up a new notion of multicultural identity, while at the same time there are new racisms which 'are abroad everywhere and gaining ground' (p. 238). He points out that the celebration of the anniversary of the arrival of the *Windrush* occurred at the same time as the Macpherson Inquiry report into the death of Stephen Lawrence, a juxtaposition that is 'deeply paradigmatic of the contradictory state of British multiculturalism'.

Multicultural relationships and inter-subjectivities contain deeply contradictory states. It is, on the one hand, situated in a context of white dominance, where anyone else is other (black) and in which the ascription, black, marks a sign of resistance. They are subject to the invasive projections of racism and, more subtly, objectification, as stereotypical representatives – Hall's (1988) 'the violent avenger' is one kind of projected image of black youth, which persists in the attribution of violent deviance, not only to African Carribbean young men, but, more recently, also to the Asian gang (Alexander 2000). 'Celebratory multiculturalism', for example, highly valuing ethnic food, objectifies and disguises the experiences of contested, racist intersubjective encounters (Parker 2000). Particularly in the realm of the body, sport and sexuality, the projection of the 'hyper-physicality' of the black body produces a 'celebratory' image, which masks denigratory undertones. In these encounters 'the shadow of the Other falls upon the Self' (Bhabha 1990).

As well as these risks and hazards, there are new opportunities in multicultural contexts. Young people are influenced by those who 'speak a new language of hybridity and diaspora, neither torn between two cultures nor simply one or the other, but complex dynamic fusions' (Bhattacharyya and Gabriel 1997). The consciousness of these self-definitions stands for the adoption of the need that, in diasporic conditions, 'people are often obliged to adopt shifting, multiple or hyphenated positions of identification . . . even where the more traditionally orientated sections (of society) are concerned the principle of heterogeneity continues to be strongly operative' (Hall 2000). Hall gives typological examples of 'hybridity': 'the black teenager who is a dance-hall DJ, plays jungle music but supports Manchester United, or the Muslim student who wears baggy, hip-hop, street style jeans but is never absent from Friday prayers'.

But, he also adds that hybridity does not describe an individual, 'who can be contrasted as fully-formed subjects with "traditionals" and "moderns"'. Within the process of hyphenation or hybridity there are possibilities for transformation, which make a distinction between traditional and modern inadequate in that they produce fixed, inaccurate stereotypes. Hall refers to Homi Bhabha's discussion of the 'ambiguous, anxious moment of transition' as

> not simply appropriation or adaptation, it is a process through which cultures are required to revise their own systems of reference, norms and values by departing from their habitual or 'inbred' rules of transformation. Ambivalence and antagonism accompany any act of cultural translation because negotiating with the 'difference of the other' reveals the radical insufficiency of our own systems of meaning and signification. (Bhabha 1997)

Adolescents face their own quests for identity within two over-lapping processes, in which individual and cultural identity are both decentred. The ethnic minority adolescent's struggle is subject to adaptation and assimilation to and within a 'host' culture. The host adolescent, because of dominance, has more choice. Relinquishing a position of centredness, with all the privileges it seems to confer, is based more on depressive qualities of being able and willing to accept and tolerate difference, without foreclosing in negative, racist, or celebratory multiculturalism. In practical terms, therapeutic work with adolescents from minority ethnic backgrounds involves the therapist in complex ways of making sense of the individual within her/his culture, and the relationship between the adolescent and her/himself.

Case example: Azma

Azma, 18, an Egyptian woman, came to therapy feeling depressed and unable to study or participate in class, where she became intransigently silent. She began her therapy energetically, striking up a good rapport and feeling understanding of and relief from her depression. She began to be able to study again and to speak in class. Not speaking became a major theme, for as well as not speaking in class she told me she did not speak to her father. During this silence I would try to say what I felt may be the current meaning of her silence, and she would from time to time indicate her agreement or not by turning her head either towards me, or away from me. She did, verbally, indicate agreement that she was worried about keeping or losing control. As she began to be more articulate she exerted control by insisting on choosing what she would talk about and refusing to entertain discussion of any other subject, that is, she would not respond to me if I used anything other than the exact words she had used.

In these circumstances, a working theory is extremely useful. Britton (1998) in his work on 'triangular space' has developed a way of thinking about the problem of difference, through discussion of situations where it seems difficult for someone to accept a different perspective. The capacity for tolerating different perspectives arises from the early relationship between the infant and the parents:

If a link between the parents is perceived in love and hate can be tolerated in the child's mind it provides the child with a prototype for an object relationship of a third kind in which he or she is a witness and not a participant. A third position then comes into existence from which object relationships can be observed. Given this we can also envisage being observed. This provides us with a capacity for seeing ourselves in interaction with others and for entertaining another point of view while retaining our own – for observing ourselves while being ourselves. I call the mental freedom provided by this process triangular space. (1998 p. 42)

The problem for those patients in analysis who cannot tolerate the third position is that the idea of another point of view is overwhelming, and threatens obliteration of the self. Any approach to a different perspective is usually met with withdrawal or violence. Britton suggests that technically at this point the only way to proceed is to demonstrate understanding of the patient's point of view, by putting it into words. This calms the patient, and provides a sense of understanding, but not collusion or agreement. The need for agreement, Britton argues, becomes insistent when disagreement needs to be annihilated. He proposes a 'general rule':

the need for agreement is inversely proportional to the expectation of understanding. When expectation of understanding is high, difference of opinion is tolerable; when expectation of understanding is fairly high, difference is fairly tolerable; when there is no expectation of understanding, the need for agreement is absolute. (p. 57)

In this way Britton links the capacity for tolerance of difference with the experience of containment, so that the capacity to tolerate different perspectives marks a freedom or flexibility internally, in which agreement is not felt to be imperative. The greater degree of internal freedom implies greater separateness and a capacity to relinquish control of the other. If we add to this the context of adolescent identity formation, the capacity to occupy the 'third position' facilitates the capacity to move between subject positions. The acceptance of links between other people, and within others' minds, mirrors the movement between different subject positions.

The problem of difference between Azma and myself can be stated in external or social terms. Whereas she was Egyptian, Muslim, female and adolescent, I am white British, male, adult and my upbringing was Christian. In the relationship with her I also came to hold, or contain, the problems that were so difficult to discuss, that affected her in her family and school. The intensity of her silence and need for me to agree with her increased as she obtained greater freedom in her family and school.

How is it possible to account for these experiences of Azma in her therapy? Her silence seemed on one level to have the quality of repetition, so that her father, her tutor and I at different times experienced this silence. It also seemed to be the case that when the silence became located in her therapy she became freer in her other, external situations, her family and school. It is true her silence was a furious one, though this did not explain why she was furious. She was able to stay in therapy, and listen to my thoughts, as she was silent, occasionally indicating agreement, and when I spoke about her need to be in control, and her fear of it, she spoke in agreement. But there seemed to be something very important missing. I could say to her 'look, there's silence here, like there was silence at school and at home, and we can try and think together about this', yet this was not possible, until, indirectly, she brought material which expressed her position in cultural terms that more openness was possible:

> She talked to me over a number of sessions about two groups of school-friends. One group was focused on homework, the other on parties and going out. She was a member of the homework group, but she also wanted to be in the party group. On one occasion she told me that at lunchtime she went to sit with the party group. Then she saw that there was only one member of the homework group, and she felt awful that she had left this girl on her own. To compound her misery the girls in the party group asked her, rather rejectingly, what she was doing joining them. She said she would not to do that again.

It seemed very clear that the homework and party groups represented two aspects of herself, or two identifications she would like to have. She did not mention the ethnicity of the members of the two groups, but she seemed to convey that the homework group was mainly Asian, or Muslim. Two more significant features occurred to me. Firstly, there was the sense of a part of herself who felt left and abandoned (like the girl in the homework group) and second, she had the utmost difficulty moving between the two positions represented by the two groups.

Azma demonstrated a difficulty in moving between subject positions through her extremely constrained way of relating to me in her therapy. There was tremendous difficulty in discussing some apparently straightforward issues, particularly with regard to descriptive issues about the impact of her cultural background on her life within her family, at school and in her therapy. Azma's therapy became extremely important to her, and became for her the means whereby she had been able to become more successful in the cross-cultural domain of school. When she was more confident in speaking in her therapy, she spoke about how she was constrained severely by her parents in where she could go and whom she could see, and now her parents would not countenance dating. Ultimately, she said, she expected that a marriage would be arranged for her, but she did not think about it much. The forbidden external – dating – was mirrored by the way she dealt with her own feelings about sex and sexuality by *not* thinking.

Azma became increasingly aware of belonging to her parents' culture, but feeling able to negotiate within that sphere, and alongside this she became more confident and less agonised in her peer relationships. Though she often had a feeling of being misunderstood, and she dreaded abandonment and rejection, she did develop a new kind of relation with herself, which was both rooted in her parents' culture and different from her parents.

Strong cultural ties

Azma felt that she was able to reach a point in which she could have a sense of relating both within her family and across the cultural boundary. These positions were continuously changing, and agonised. In the reflective way in which she looked at herself in own culture, she felt able to draw on its strengths. Azma was able to get hold of a sense of belonging, in a strong culture.

Hall (2000) illustrates the idea of the strong ties of an ethnic nature in Asian and Afro-Caribbean communities through quoting Parekh (1991). Strong ties are

> ethnic in nature, that is, physically distinguishable, bonded by social ties arising out of shared customs, language and practice of inter-marriage and having their distinct history, collective memories, geographical origins, views of life and modes of social organisation.

But also, at the same time, there is a sense of turbulence:

> Great changes are afoot within ethnic communities and every family has become a terrain of subdued or explosive struggles. In every family, husband and wife, parents and children, brothers and sisters are having to re-negotiate and re-define their patterns of relationship in a manner that takes account both of traditional values and those characteristic of their adopted country. Different families reach their own inherently tentative conclusions. (Hall 2000, pp. 220–1)

The idea of a strong culture, and maintaining a place within it – that is, identifying with it or feeling a sense of belonging with it – is helpful to adolescents. Though the ground is in motion in terms of the changes within families, the capacity to think about and relate to a culture, which is substantial, but also alive and changing, is distinctly advantageous. Parekh indicates the robustness of having traditions, facing change and becoming different.

Adolescents are affected by attacks on their culture through the negative experiences of racism, and this can bring about closer attachments with family and other same culture contacts as a protective withdrawal under the persecutory conditions of racism. Second, the family's history and experience of migration affect adolescents, and especially if the circumstances are traumatic. But there is loss in every transition and migration. Eisenbruch (1990) has referred to the idea of 'cultural bereavement' when there is disruption through migration. Bains (2001) points out that the meaning of migration and the quality of loss experienced by adolescents in their families needs to be understood. For example, this may be experienced by the absence of, especially, the father returning to the home country. She also evidences the way that loss of home is especially by disillusion in the new country, especially by experiences of racism. Sometimes, adolescents become adrift from their families and an acute sense of not belonging ensues.

A sense of belonging

Becoming stuck or frozen without a sense of belonging is most likely to cause serious difficulties. Noam (1999) has argued that a sense of belonging is an important component of adolescent development, and one which stands to some extent opposed to the 'task' of developing a coherent, integrated identity; 'to yearn for belonging is to be able to risk relationship and loss' (p. 61). If this yearning is exaggerated then masochism, loss of self and an easily exploited social conformity result. Rather than achieving an integrated and solitary identity, the need is 'the capacity to belong to multiple worlds, to live with them and to be able to travel between them' (p. 60) through maintaining contact with these worlds, rather than feeling excluded from them. Noam gives an example of a 19-to-20-year-old in therapy following a serious suicidal attempt:

> Rosa did not fit in with her family, nor did she fit in at college. She attempted to develop intimate relationships but this led a to a series of brief sexual relationships which left her feeling vulnerable and hateful towards herself. As a child in her family and as a student, Rosa felt she was between two worlds and belonged to neither. She decided to travel, with the purpose of setting up events for the college's alumni association, and Noam understood that with this plan she became a worker, maintaining her connections with both the college and her family. Through rearranging the context in which she lived, Rosa shifted her subject position. Noam discusses the implications for therapy: 'I remember the dramatic moment when she came to my office with flowers to announce that she was leaving for an indefinite amount of time, maybe even forever.' But Rosa was clear that she would stay in touch and her case should not be considered 'closed'. Noam agreed that it was important to allow this, because 'part of the need to belong is to continue to belong during separations', despite the administrative and audit anxieties this created in the organisation, an apt example of the conflict working with adolescents places on organisational norms.

Noam sees adolescents like Rosa as 'seeking contexts of affirmation' in order to take up subject positions which 'rearrange the context' in which they live (p. 60). This is in turn predicated on the history of insecure attachments that adolescents seeking therapy bring, and the impact on adolescent development of these histories.

Hall (2000) refers to Habermas, writing of political intersubjectivity, saying

> From a normative point of view the integrity of the individual legal person cannot be guaranteed without protecting the inter-subjectively shared experiences and life contexts in which the person has been socialized and formed his or her identity. The identity of the individual is interwoven with collective identities and can be stabilized only in a cultural network that cannot be appropriated as private property, any more than the mother tongue itself can. Hence the individual remains the bearer of 'rights to cultural membership'. (Habermas 1994)

This speaks to the priority of an unalienable cultural belonging, cuts through the dichotomy of individual–collective (Hall 2000, p. 231), and is particularly interesting in that it addresses the problem of sharing. The bedrock of identity in a culture, a language and the 'intersubjectively shared experiences and life contexts' is a precondition for sharing across cultures. This is a position which is fairly close to the view Stern (1985) puts forward about the infant's capacity to intersubjectively share mental states, which is that the infant needs to experience the 'attuned' mother paying attention to the infant's communicative rhythms. Without this there is foreclosure, and communication with others, including across cultures, excludes difference. This, in terms of adolescent identity and subjectivity, is extremely important, that a shift between subject positions is predicated on a 'secure base' or an experience of containment. This can be put very simply. Difference is not tolerable without enough sameness. A sense of sameness, or identification, begins to be developed in early infancy, and not only is about the taking in by another of the emotions that are too difficult to bear within oneself, but also is predicated on the way the parent or container returns these experiences. Often this is thought of as mirroring, a reflecting back of 'sameness', but it is more subtle than this. The 'mirroring' process includes an element of difference through differentiation of self and other, in qualities that are bearable. This requires a great sensitivity. Sameness and difference are not things, or just polarised opposites (though they can be); they are 'positional along a spectrum' and in dynamic relation with each other. The importance and subtleties of understanding the meaning of what is projected, and what can be fed back, mean that therapists have to work very hard within a reflective psycho-social space when working with issues of ethnic identity with adolescents. It means tolerating and thinking about meaning in a context that is ambiguous, painful and often precarious, even fragile. It is very important to have space for the meanings that emerge from the socio-cultural space because

> psychotherapy undertaken with young adults ... suggests that cross-cultural factors may have a significant effect in the development of self-autonomy, the formation of a self-identity and the acceptance of a sexual self. (Bains 2001, p. 73)

Summary

- In this chapter ethnic identity formation in adolescence was explored. Ethnic identity makes a significant contribution to overall identity formation and subjectivity.
- The space in which ethnic identity develops is subject to forces that operate across socio-cultural and psychic domains, creating a complex, ambiguous context for therapeutic work with adolescents.
- Negative experiences – racism – are very significant for identity formation in adolescence, and minority ethnic adolescents are involved in precarious processes of engaging at a cross-cultural level. Withdrawal into same culture groups may be a consequence of experiencing racism. Adolescents have to face considerable difficulties in trying to negotiate and survive these experiences
- White adolescents who cannot tolerate the experience of difference defend against this by splitting and projecting in order to maintain the semblance (delusion) of a powerful, oppressive sameness. The psychic roots of racism are very deep, and infantile. They are closely connected with inability to face the loss of separation, and thus are very active in adolescence.

- There are risks and hazards and opportunities in multicultural contacts. The discussion of hybridity focuses on one of these ambiguous possibilities, in the context of individuals and cultures being in agonised flux.
- Case examples illustrate the qualities, difficulties, ambiguities and fragilities of therapeutic contact with adolescents. The importance of containment, mirroring, a sense of belonging, and the capacity to take into account meaning at a socio-cultural level are important in facilitating therapeutic work.

4

PARENTING ADOLESCENTS

This chapter explores the way adolescents and their parents relate to each other in contexts of change and diversity. The emphasis in this discussion is placed on how anxiety from within and around the adolescent impacts on families, and, second, how the impact of loss, which arises in parent–adolescent relationships in many ways, leads to difficulties, and possibilities, of mourning. The complexities of changes in structure, values and authority in families and how these affect parenting of adolescents are also discussed.

The intensity of parenting adolescents

There is some consensus, from different viewpoints, that a capacity in parents to move between the adolescent's fluctuating states of mind and positioning helps retain receptivity and communication. Coleman and Hendry (1999) show that a parental capacity to connect with the intensity of emotions is an important constituent of maintaining connection in relationships, as, too, is the ability to renegotiate relationships. Anderson emphasises that 'there is a fluctuation between the need to use parents as temporary recipients of projections and the ability to contain anxiety and be more independent' (1999 p. 166). Moving between different relational positions, being responsive now to the need to allow the adolescent to try to contain emotional states in her/himself, now to the need for the parent to act as a container of unmanageable feelings, makes parenting of adolescents demanding. The difficulty of parenting lies in the intensity of feelings, which are projected on to parental figures. Anderson sums up this difficulty:

> Sometimes it feels as though all the unwanted feelings, hopelessness, incompetence, and fear on the one hand, and responsibility and worry without the power to go with it on the other, are left with the parents. (1999 p. 166)

Therefore it is important to think how certain qualities of relationship make for developmental possibilities in adolescence, and, alternatively, those which lead to developmental difficulties. It is also important to assess how the turbulence and diversity of the contemporary social context affect the relationships between adolescents and parental figures.

Case example: Jamie

Mrs F had approached her GP because she was worried about her son Jamie, who was now 13. She had told the GP that Jamie's behaviour had deteriorated, especially at school, where he was often in trouble. At a recent meeting at school with his teachers, she had been told that he was at risk of suspension from school, because of his aggression towards other students, his noncompliance with authority, and because he had been increasingly not turning up for lessons. Additionally, Jamie's parents had been told that it had been suspected he had been involved with using drugs. Mrs F had told her GP that Jamie was increasingly uncommunicative at home, and that there were frequent arguments between Jamie and his father. She had felt that the problems had been gradually getting worse over the past two years and that Jamie had never really settled into his secondary school. However, she had been at a loss to know what was causing these difficulties, and though worried about Jamie she 'did not know what was the matter with him' nor could she or anyone else 'get through to him'. She had a daughter two years younger than Jamie who was not causing any concern. She had asked the GP if there was someone Jamie could see, who might accomplish what she could not, and 'get through to him'.

At this point the GP had the problem of deciding how to proceed with Mrs F's request. She could either suggest that mother spend some time with the practice's counsellor talking this through in some more detail (Wiener and Sher 1998), she could agree to mother's request to refer Jamie for a therapeutic consultation, or she could suggest that the family have a therapeutic consultation together. Alternatively, she could suggest that Mrs F, either alone or with Mr F and perhaps also Jamie, meet with teachers again to try to find ways of resolving these difficulties, and it might be that the school had a counsellor attached who could see Jamie. However, one missing aspect was that the GP has not seen Jamie, nor did she know how Jamie might view any of these options, especially those that involved him in attending meetings or therapeutic consultations. More information would help, but the GP had a knife-edge decision to make, and this would depend to some extent on the way Mrs F impacted upon her. If Mrs F communicated an urgency and insistence about Jamie being seen, it might be difficult to propose alternatives without becoming embroiled in complicated discussions.

The situation had the hallmarks of a narrative about a 'folk devil' (Cohen 1973) in the making; an uncommunicative, aggressive male adolescent, who was beyond comprehension, was suspected of turning to drugs. There was worry about Jamie, and possibly worry for him, which already has spread across three institutions – the family, the school and the GP practice – and might shortly encompass a fourth – an organisation offering therapeutic consultation to adolescents and their families. Let us continue with the case:

> The GP ascertained from Mrs F that Jamie knew of this meeting, and that Jamie was willing to attend a therapeutic consultation. She then referred Jamie to a therapeutic service, and an appointment was sent to Jamie. He did not attend, but shortly before the end of the hour offered for the appointment, mother telephones the agency and speaks with the therapist. She said Jamie was not willing to attend and she was worried that he would have lost his chance for help. She communicated an urgent worry, amounting to fearfulness at the lost opportunity. She said he really did need help and yet he was so stubborn about not attending. She had made it clear she would come with him and wait for him but he would still not come. After some discussion, taking into account mother's urgency, the therapist offered an appointment for them both. Mother said she thought it might work if father came too, and the therapist agreed to a consultation with all three. They attended.
>
> At this meeting, Mrs F began by reiterating her concerns about Jamie, speaking about how difficult it was to talk to him and how difficult he

was to understand. She spoke of his difficulties in school, and what his teachers had told her about him. As she proceeded, she asked Jamie to confirm that each was true. Jamie lowered his head and did not reply until Mrs F mentioned the allegation of drug dealing and then Jamie retorted 'I never'. The atmosphere developed into that resembling a courtroom, in which Jamie was firmly placed in the witness box, and he responded by putting the case for the defence. When asked what he thought about coming, Jamie said that he did not mind but he would not come on his own. He added that he thought everything was being exaggerated and there was nothing that needed to be done, but his parents, especially his mother, worried a lot.

Then Mr F, with barely controlled fury, spoke of his many grievances about his son, who, he was convinced, would end up in a lot of trouble. He said that Jamie humiliated him by not taking his advice and that he never complied with father's wishes. For example, Mr F said that he had asked Jamie to meet him at a certain place and time and when Jamie did not appear, father felt 'left high and dry'. Jamie's shoulders hunched and he turned away, looking at the floor, as father was talking. Mrs F invited father to tell the therapist about the time he chased Jamie out of the house and down the street. Father retorted that Mrs F should tell this story; both Mr F and Jamie seemed embarrassed. Mrs F then said she felt something had to be done, but that she had no idea what this might be; she was at her wits' end, and she just hoped Jamie might open up to someone outside the situation. A feeling began to emerge, unspoken, that they felt the consultation was going to be futile. She added that he had been a difficult child, especially when a baby, but she had thought he had grown out of this before the present difficulties began. She hoped that it would not have an effect on Sharon, Jamie's sister, who was 10 and who had been no trouble at all so far.

The therapist, feeling that anything she said might confirm one or more members of the family as failing, and that she could add to their worry, fury and embarrassment, was under pressure to act as judge in this courtroom atmosphere. In fact she suggested that the difficulties needed careful consideration, and asked the parents to meet again. Jamie was offered the choice of attending if he felt he wished to, with the understanding that his presence would be welcomed, but that he might have thoughts about whether he preferred the therapist and the parents to talk in his presence or in his absence about his situation.

Jamie's identity, as not communicating or understandable, generated anxiety in his parents, who with increasing forcefulness tried to gain access to him, through 'chasing' after him and focusing on requests to get him to 'open up'.

All four members of the family had adopted subjective positions, or 'stances', with which they identify, in a paranoid-schizoid field. Mother was worried, but unable to find inside herself a way of making contact with Jamie, who was felt to be as much causing difficulties as being in need of understanding. Father had grievances about Jamie and expressed these aggressively – both verbally and by 'chasing' after him. Sharon was identified as absent, and as not having difficulties. Jamie was both a victim of parental not understanding and provocative to his parents,[1] and it seemed evident that he knew his behaviour would successfully 'wind up' his father. In the consultation, Jamie did not respond to his father's complaints, except to noticeably turn away from him. His expression seemed to shut father out and to increase the intensity of controlled humiliation and rage. It seemed that father and son were on a collision course, and that Jamie's strategy of running away was in effect goading father, and projecting his fury into him. From a different perspective, his relationships with his father appeared to mirror, and reverse, the relationships Jamie had at school, where he was also thought of as not complying with authority, but also of 'chasing after' other students. There was an escalating and progressively distorting picture emerging of the relationships in the family and in the wider network, in which adults were becoming 'infected' by the feelings of helplessness and a punitive wish to take control.

Anxiety and positioning in families of adolescents

Where anxiety is high, and the availability of a reflective thoughtful containment is impaired, there is both a 'contagion' and concreteness in the projection of anxiety, originating from and/or instigated by the presence of an adolescent. In the F family, in the absence of connectedness and understanding, something, which seems to focus on the difficulties of male adolescence, begins to run through the family, the school and then into other institutions. Mrs F experiences anxiety passively, as brought about by Jamie's behaviour. Mr F has an identity as trying to catch and control the elusive Jamie.

The image of Mr F pursuing Jamie is an apt metaphor for 'chasing' adolescents, through the impact of anxiety that leads to a fear of losing control. Mrs F's passive not understanding is paradigmatic of a position in which all the difficulty of adolescence is located in the adolescent. In contrast, in a reflective, containing space, adults permit themselves to be 'used' by the adolescent for the projection into them of emotions and states of mind, in order to find meaning in what is unknown or uncertain.

Jamie's position was also paradigmatic of relationships between adolescents and adults, in that he projected worry and aggression into his parents, in the hope or expectation that these feelings will be taken in. In this situation the problem includes the parental feeling that Jamie is not understandable. Adolescents require parents to move between two positions; first, the position in which they are negotiable, and manage, or aim to manage, their emotional responsibilities within themselves, and expect to be negotiated with. Second, they need the parent to take in the emotionality, which they cannot manage themselves, and to think about its meaning with and for them. Different states of mind need containment, over time and in different adolescents. It is highly important that the different needs of parents are not muddled, since the adolescent's new developments stem from the capacity to respond to times and issues which they manage emotionally within the self. Differentiating these from states of mind which require a particularly difficult or dangerous aspect of the self, understood by someone alongside oneself, is an important parental function.

The absence or constriction of the negotiable side of things is indicative of difficulties in the transition from childhood to adolescence, and, socially, from primary to secondary school. The anxiety that is thus mobilised, and not contained, becomes contagious and distortable and is highly likely to escalate.

Changing families

Processes of accelerating social change have created new diversities, and among the most significant of these are a new range of family structures, models and cultural values. These new models of families emerge tentatively and provisionally. Differences of languages, histories, and customs create newness, change and complex levels of conflict between tradition and newness. For example, there is an increase in families headed by a lone parent, and an increasing number of adolescents have lived in a family in which change in a parenting relationship has taken place. More children are born outside marriage and 'conventional notions of marriage are being replaced by more fluid relationship structures' (Coleman and Hendry 1999, p. 87). Dartington (1998) points out there are at least three categories of single parents, who derive their positions from bereavement, divorce and being single, and that these positions have different meanings for the parent. Adolescents will therefore experience different family structures, and also, in some cases, during childhood and adolescence they will have experience of more than one family structure. Families may separate and reconstitute, so that both the loss of a family relationship and the arrival of new family members will take place. The birth of babies and new partners and their children are both in this category of new arrivals. Thus in thinking about adolescents' experiences of families, one must not only be aware of structure and structural changes, but also understand something of the quality of the context, and the changes. Is there a painful or unthinkable loss? What kinds of conflicts are alive in the family? Is it possible that there are benefits and opportunities brought by changes? Are emotional experiences of change, and loss, processed in the family, to some extent at least?

In these conditions, there is no centre or solidity; instead of a reliable and predictable model of a family there is unpredictability and risk. The family in the mind and the family in social reality may be quite different entities. The problem for adolescents in this context is that their involvement in the individual and internal changes of adolescence has to be experienced and worked through in the context of a changing and unpredictable world. The parents and carers of adolescents have to be able to maintain a capacity to make contact with the emotionality of adolescents, to make and maintain links between the past, present and future when they themselves are in a process of turbulent change. This is demanding, and yet the task of parenting adolescence is itself demanding, emotionally and mentally, since adolescents, despite perhaps protestations to the contrary, have great need of parents, who can contain the intensity of emotions and make contact in a negotiable way. In exploring relationships between parents, carers and adolescents, the themes of control and fear of loss of control, and the difficulties of mourning, are to the forefront.

Families of adolescents

Changes to the family, the increase in lone-parent families and the multiplicity of models of the family pose real problems for traditional theories of family relationships. As Dartington (1998) has noted, 'traditional literature is full of warnings about what happens to children who are separated from the idealised, balanced, containing couple' (p. 14). Britton (1989) developed the idea of the 'third' position, where there is a reflective space in the mind in which there are internal connections and links. Thus if the parent can draw on this reflective capacity internally, through representations of good, helpful and sustaining relationships with others, an internal couple is in existence. In practice most parents need to draw on others in the external world to make a reflective and containing connection, or link. The case illustrations in this chapter show the way therapeutic consultation can be used as a reflective space, in order to develop the capacity for thinking about emotionality.

Case example: Simone

Simone, 16, had a restricted social existence. She was interested and motivated to succeed in her schoolwork, but she had no friends and no social life outside the home. Her rather defensive view of his isolation from peers was that she could not find anyone who was like-minded, meaning serious and academic. Simone's father had become very worried about her and came with her for therapeutic consultations.

Simone's mother had some time ago eloped and now lived abroad with her new husband. Father had a girlfriend, who stayed with them some of the time, but did not seem very committed to the relationship. Simone's older brother, Michael, was now near the end of his first year at university, living away from home most of the time. With all these absences, father and Simone felt stuck together, as she put it, 'like two monkeys in a cage'. It was very difficult for either of them to think about becoming more separate from each other, and they put their hopes in the passage of time providing a solution.

Frequently, father would talk about setting a boundary between them, or about acting independently of Simone, only to sabotage these thoughts. On one occasion he found himself with some time and went to a bookshop. He said he could have spent all day there, but then became worried about Simone and phoned her.

For her part, Simone expected and demanded open access to father, including access to his bedroom. On occasions she got into bed to 'have a cuddle'. It seemed unlikely that any sexual enactments took place, and Simone exerted terrific control over her desires and needs through intense exercise and a low-calorie diet.

There was, between Simone and her father, an intolerable sense of depression and a dread of separateness, which had to be avoided. This was closely linked with problem of emotionality in this pair that difficult feelings had to be quickly left behind. Father, sadly and rather tragically, talked about his childhood and adolescence:

He described a 'disastrous' marriage between his parents, and a mother who had been very depressed. When he spoke of his father he said he was 'sadly relieved' when he died, because he had made him jump through hoops. His siblings, a brother and a sister, had had problems, and his sister had emigrated. Simone's father had spent many years responsible for the care of his depressed mother after his father's death.

Father seemed to long for a relationship which might offer the possibility not just of enduring difficulty and depression, but also of sustaining a hope of repairing or transforming these experiences. His awareness of missing this kind of relationship with another person, and inside himself, appeared to free Simone from the role she had of telling him to 'pull himself together and get on with it' when he was depressed. Instead Simone began to speak of missing a 'mother who she could go shopping with', a very 'ordinary' relationship and the kind she usually shunned.

In the relationship, both Simone and her father were stuck, or frozen, in a way that seemed fateful. Bollas (1991) has made a distinction between fate and destiny. The 'fated' individual is acted upon by forces to which s/he has to follow a script. In contrast, 'destiny' can be made, or carved, or reached for, and involves active authorship or agency:

> A person who is fated, who is fundamentally interred in an internal world of self and object relationships that endlessly repeat the same scenarios, has very little sense of a future that is at all different from the internal environment they carry around with them. The sense of fate is a feeling of despair to influence the course of one's life. A sense of destiny, however, is a different state, when the person feels he is moving in a personality progression that gives him a sense of steering his course. (Bollas 1991 p. 41)

When Simone and her father were able to bear the painfulness of what has been missed and lost, a different position emerged, in which there were new possibilities and a greater openness. These followed from a more active engagement with internal processes (destiny) – rather than being fated to follow a repetitious and circumscribed closure.

Becoming caught up in grievances and resentments is a defence against mourning and also against awareness. These occur, often, in families with adolescents when a painful separation is involved. Parental separation, unless the parents emotionally digest the experience, creates vulnerability for difficulties in development, in the triangle of mother, father and adolescent. Feeling injured can lead to grievance, revenge or, through awareness of damage, reparation. Steiner (1993) has argued that revenge 'is a complex phenomenon' in that, in taking revenge, there is an attempt to 'stand up and against those who injure us and threaten our objects' (p. 85). Thus revenge may indicate the presence of a capacity to face experience rather than evade it, through harbouring resentment and grievances. On the other hand, revenge, though illustrating an awareness of pain, is also a way of evading the overwhelming impact of damage for which no reparation seems possible.

There are problems between mothers and sons in circumstances such as the case of Simone and her father, of finding appropriate boundaries to permit separateness, and also to acknowledge that adolescent sexuality requires different boundaries than in earlier childhood. In both father–daughter and mother–son relationships there can be a difficulty in the regulation of intimacy and distance.

Sayers (1991) gives an example of a father in Carson McCullers's novel *The Member of the Wedding* who becomes insensitive with his daughter through feeling uncomfortable with the need to redefine the relationship between them, as his daughter reaches puberty:

> Who is this great big long-legged twelve year old blunderbuss who still wants to sleep with her old papa . . . She began to have a grudge against her father and they looked at each other in a slant-eyed way. (Quoted in Sayers 1991, p. 76)

Different parents

In contexts of diversity, adolescents may have to endure, and be able to make sense of, very different images of parents. The idealisation of the 1950s family, with father at work and mother in the kitchen, is thus replaced by complex and contradictory images of parents. Changes in family patterns and families being in processes of repeated change and reconstitution means that adolescents are more exposed, not only to separation, loss and uncertainty, but also to different parental lifestyles and parental sexuality. In the idealised family, parental sex is firmly behind closed doors, so that at the extreme it is invisible. Adolescents are free in these circumstances to generate the illusion that parental sex is no longer an active issue. In more turbulent contexts, parents may appear 'wacky' to their adolescents. One 15-year-old boy described the sense of embarrassment he felt when his young mother of 33 attended parents' evenings at school dressed in a short skirt and a leather jacket. He said, in resignation, that she was always out, at work and with friends, that they lived on ready-made meals from Sainsbury's, and that he sometimes wished he 'had a mother in an apron'. The *Independent* reported this at the Reading festival:

> One woman in her forties with five nose rings and a lip stud had no qualms about dancing . . . By shaking maniacally like a dog as it leaves the sea. Then she said to her daughter of about 10 in a delightful sub-

urban mumsy voice 'Jeanette, if you can't behave I'm taking you home and you won't see Eminem.' (*Independent*, 28 August 2001)

The account is intended to sound wacky, and contrasts, journalistically, images of mothers that seem incongruent. More seriously, a young woman of 19 complained to me that 'my mother's got a new boyfriend and it's doing my head in'. With a definite attempt at establishing her superiority, she added that her mother was 'going on about her new boyfriend and her ex-husband, and it reminds me how I used to be, always having two boyfriends'.

It seems imperative to differentiate the wacky from the destructive, and the different from the perpetrating of damaging and abusive experiences. Early adolescents find it difficult to think about their parent's lives – and this is one of the differentiating, separating struggles of adolescence, to gain a sense of perspective about parents in place of childhood idealisations and distortions. This is a painful, difficult and anxious process. Adolescents dislike having to deal with the detail of parents' lives, and then to have to contain within themselves ideas about parents as they are, in their lives, with roles other than parenting. One 18-year-old found it difficult to gain a sense of herself as separate from her mother. Her mother had been very lonely and depressed when she was young and had wanted to involve her daughter in her life as a support for her. This led to the girl having to listen to the details of her mother's current relationship dilemmas.

Tom's parents were in conflict because his father had had an affair. Tom – 15 – was devastated by this knowledge and felt his world had been turned upside down. His previously admired father became synonymous with betrayal, disillusion and contempt. Tom complained furiously, with unconscious humour, that it was a burden having a father who 'always screwed up'. Tom was swept from childhood idealisation of his father to intense disillusionment in a way which was too intense and too sudden for him to accommodate. He seemed to not be able, within himself, to mediate the impact of this on his inner world and the effect was traumatic. Other adolescents may, in different circumstances, have adapted to this experience in different ways. These examples may be thought of as coming within a category of difficult experiences for the adolescent to digest and come to terms with. More extreme is the exposure to aspects of parental behaviour, including parental sexuality, which can be damaging, destructive and abusive.

Case example: Josie

Josie, 18, initially told me that her mother was eccentric, and that she had many problems and neglected her. The relationship had got much worse during adolescence and Josie had moved out to live with a friend's family. This produced complex and ambivalent feelings, in that Josie felt relieved not to be living with mother but also guilty at leaving her. She had a tendency to discuss mother in extreme terms as extremely bizarre and monstrous, or ideally anticipating Josie's needs and wishes. Josie thus talked about perfectly idealised times when she and mother were fused together, and this included going out together, dressed alike. On the other side of this extreme split, Josie had memories of mother leaving her at home as a small child while mother went out to drink and party, and times when mother would return home with a sequence of boyfriends.

The unpredictability of Josie's environment, which threatened her sense of internal continuity, left her with difficulties in maintaining intimate relationships and also in being separate. She idealised the times when mother was 'in tune' with her, and also seemed to be (unconsciously) identified with her when her behaviour mirrored the way she talked about mother. Josie had difficulties in separating from mother internally, and from recognising difference between them, which she experienced as extremes – ideal or awful. In these circumstances, the adolescent is left with a difficult task of developing a sense of identity, which is separate from parental figures. To mourn the loss of parents and childhood that one wished one had had is a difficult emotional task, made extremely onerous by the impact of disturbance and difficulty in the parents which has been inflicted upon or projected into the adolescent. Adolescents in these circumstances may become very defended and stuck in their development, or encounter a difficult range of emotional experiences, in which hate and resentment, grievances about the parent, and fear of their own emotionality feature strongly. In each case, a detailed exploration of the relationship and its meaning for the adolescent is necessary in order to facilitate the process of mourning.

Parents in pain about adolescents

The process of parenting adolescents means being in touch with a particular pain of separation, in which adolescence marks the beginning of the end of childhood, and in which the ultimate loss of the relationship is conceptualised in the anticipation of the adolescent leaving home. This stirs up in parents their past experiences of separation and loss. The fear of not being in control is activated in both adolescents and their parents because the process of change in adolescence is driven by inevitability. Individually and culturally, defences against this loss are also activated. In parents, the experience of separating from the adolescent can reactivate infantile feelings of the fear of loss. It is of course a function of parenting to worry about the adolescent's emerging adulthood, and increased independence, and to think about this anxiety and take a perspective on it, attempting to evaluate the risks and hazards involved. In conditions of modernity many of these risks and hazards will be new, and will not relate to parental socio-cultural experiences. Change occurs more quickly in the socio-cultural sphere than in the internal world, which has to contend with the conservatism of the internalisation of values from the parents' parents' generation. Transgenerational differences are complex. The cultural inheritance of the child is also based on the past, through internalising the parents' internal parents and their values and socio-cultural worlds. Parents have internalised past values and attitudes that appropriated to past conditions. Parents may say, for example, that they draw on their experiences of parenting, which 'never did them any harm' as a way of communicating loyalty to this kind of internalisation, and also of avoiding the anxiety and confusion that arises with contemporary processes of change and turbulence.[2]

Internal authority lags behind contemporary conditions, and this can be destabilising of parenting in conditions of rapid social change, where the process of individualisation reduces links with established or traditional authority. Contemporary partner relationships may be conceptualised as fragile, owing to increasing diversity and also the retreat from traditional authorities, for example with regard to marriage, and, as a compensation for increased anxiety, the need for certainty and reassurance also increases. In contemporary conditions, parents' anxieties require internal reflection and, perhaps to a greater extent than in traditional cultures, there has to be more reliance on internal or individual authority, rather than on reference to external authorities. There is thus a process of individualisation within parenting, as Beck-Gernsheim discusses:

> Since individualisation also fosters a longing for the opposite world of intimacy, security and closeness, most people will continue to live within a partnership or family. But such ties are not the same as before, in their scope or in their degree of obligation and permanence. Out of many different strivings, longings, efforts and mistakes, out of successful and often unsuccessful experiments, a wider spectrum of the private is taking shape. As people make choices, negotiating and deciding the everyday details of do-it-yourself relationships, a 'normal chaos' of love, suffering and diversity is growing and developing. (Beck-Gernsheim 1998 p. 67)

Thus parenting takes place within a complex configuration, in which the parents' internal worlds play a very central part. Parents need to make individualised decisions; which worries and concerns about an adolescent need to be borne, and which should be acted upon? This can be an anxious process, because it involves parents in complex fields of ambiguity, uncertainty and newness. At the extremes, parents may try to eradicate risks for their adolescents, leading to the impossibility of achieving separation, or to treating all risks alike, leading to a 'sink or swim' approach to separateness and independence.

Parents have to face painful experiences of loss. These start from the process of separating, accepting the gathering independence of the adolescent, which then draws in the parents' own experiences, and challenging and testing the parents' own inner resources and capacities. Parents are more able to be in contact with their adolescents if they can recall, experience and reflect upon significant aspects of their own childhood and adolescent years. Simone's father had to mourn painfully his relationships with his parents and the relationships within his family in order to find a space internally in which she could allow Simone some separateness.

Parental experiences of socio-cultural change from their own childhood and adolescence to the contemporary adolescence of their sons and daughters need also to be thought about. The ways they have been swept along within the changes of modernity also contribute to the difficulties, and sometimes enormities, of facing loss. Simply, parents may find themselves in circumstances and qualities of relationship they had not anticipated, envisaged or thought possible. They can seem a long way from where they expected to be. Parents may have to find within themselves ways of thinking about what is different, and to be able to bear the consequent anxieties and pains.

Difficulties of mourning can thus become extremely complex, and possibly resented, reviving early experiences of 'unfairness' (Young and Gibb 1998). Grievances against their own parents, who may be felt to have given too little and inflicted losses and separations upon them as children may be stirred up. The parent has to encounter the configuration of grievance, resentment, a wish to control, and the problem of finding within a sense of perspective and reparation being imaginable and possible.

Case example: Gerry

Mrs M's son Gerry, an only child, was badly hurt in a car accident, leaving him with serious injuries. Prior to the accident, which happened when he was 17, Gerry had experienced some difficulties during his childhood and early adolescence, and there was a possibility that he was in some way partly responsible for the accident, perhaps through acting in a self-destructive way. Mrs M and Gerry's father had separated when Gerry was 13. Initially, Mrs M requested a consultation for both Gerry and herself, but Gerry did not wish to attend, and Mrs M then asked for some therapeutic meetings alone.

After Gerry's accident Mrs M was overcome with guilt about her son and devoted herself to looking after him in a compulsive way. Her relationship with Gerry deteriorated and so did Gerry's mental health. Gerry was admitted to an inpatient unit. Mrs M's guilt and panic intensified and she felt she had lost her relationship with her son, and that Gerry had lost his opportunities in life. Gerry's accident and illness were crushing to Mrs M, who had been over-involved in her son's life and her expectations of Gerry huge.

Thus, Mrs M found herself very much alone, worried about her son and herself. She told me her dreams, one of which aptly summed up her state of mind. She said she was in a warm swimming pool, alone, but then she had to leave the swimming pool and she went into the sea where a tidal wave chased her. She had to run to keep ahead of it, which she did just, but she had to keep running. Mrs M's internal world was split between idealised, peaceful and dangerous, threatening states. She felt she had been evicted from a predictable and satisfactory world into one which was unrelenting, remorseless and dangerous. Her pain and worry about her son's accident and illness were mixed with a sense of fury with Gerry, her ex-husband, and all professionals who were involved with her son. She constantly complained to and about them for, as she saw it, the inadequate treatment provided for Gerry. In her relationship with me this represented her fury that I provided 'inadequate treatment' for her, because I could not restore her world as it had been before Gerry's accident, or, to be more accurate, how she now perceived it to have been.

Alongside this constellation Mrs M talked about a conflictual relationship with her own mother, and her grievances that mother had been depriving when Mrs M was a child. She felt that she did not belong anywhere, and she identified with her parents' origins in Spain.

Painfully, Mrs M linked her grief for Gerry with her isolation in the swimming pool and she regretted that she had not taken up a more active position in the conflicts in her life. Instead of trying to confront conflictual and difficult issues, she felt that she had passively stepped back and lived her life through Gerry. She told me another dream in which she went to a party hosted by a couple who had been together through thick and thin. She found she was there with her ex-husband and wondered why she was back with him again.

The idea of a couple going through 'thick and thin' referred to the link she had made with me in her therapy, which had endured during a most difficult time in her life, when she had felt acutely alone. In providing a reflective therapeutic space in which Mrs M could think about her emotions and states of mind, she was able to gain a sense of connectedness with others. She could come out of the swimming pool and bear turbulence. In irritatingly finding herself back with her ex-husband, Mrs M could identify her tendency to repetitively seek idealised solutions. She saw that she wished to do this in her therapeutic relationship with me, which she felt should have no ending. By addressing the limits of the relationship and the similarities between her way of relating to me as well as to others, it was possible to reflect on this and to avoid the therapeutic relationship becoming another 'warm swimming pool', or idealistic retreat from the turbulence of lived experience.

Mourning, letting go of her control, omnipotence and ideali-sation led to the possibility of Mrs M facing reality and a more depressive field. Loss is experienced very deeply, and relates ultimately to the very earliest of experiences. Mrs M illustrates the quality of losses faced by contemporary parents of adoles-cents: the loss of not belonging through being dislocated from her parents' culture, the loss of her idealisation of her family of origin and of her nuclear family. Each of these tests the internal capacity to reflect and maintain an internal dialogue between past internalisations and current contexts. Srinath (1998) points out that

> survivors of trauma may sometimes be preoccupied with rescue phan-tasies or be driven by a compulsive desire to rescue others. Although this behaviour may have something genuinely reparative in it, it can also deal with the survivor's own intolerable feelings of helplessness, impo-tence, guilt and humiliation, via a projective identification into others of those feelings. (p. 143)

This can have the flavour of parents' trying to rescue themselves from the present. This puts tremendous pressure on the thera-pist, who has to bear both the loss and its impact on the parent(s), to help the parent to bear the pain, and to make sense of the context to which pain relates, in both its infantile and socio-cultural dimensions. There is also the requirement to resist the pressure to reassure too quickly, to seek instant solutions, and to 'split' into an idealised couple, which leaves the threat-ening, conflictual and unpleasant aspects outside.

Summary

- Parenting adolescence involves intensity of feeling, and requires the flexibility to move between the different posi-tions adolescents take up with regard to their development. Particularly, parents need to recognise and respond differ-ently to times when adolescents are negotiable, and attempt-ing to contain experience within themselves, and times when they need to project intense feelings into a parent, or parent figure.

- Anxiety within and about adolescents can sweep through family members and networks who are involved. In the absence of a containing, reflective space where the meaning of anxiety can be thought about, parents may take up defensive positions of passivity or trying to keep or take control.
- In the context of change and diversity, parenting models are plural, and tentative, and it is important to avoid stereotypical thinking, or putting all families within one model. The capacity to make a thoughtful reflective link internally and/or with others can forma an important sense of a 'couple' when there are single or separated parents.
- Different parents (in the sense discussed above) can create a field of uncertainty and anxiety for adolescents, alongside the anxieties emanating from internal changes in adolescence. When experiences of separation and loss are not contained by parents, difficulties in mourning arise for both parents and adolescents, and these impact on development in powerful and potentially damaging ways.
- When held in a reflective, containing space, recognition of painful experiences in the present and past provides possibilities for opening up ways of relating which enhance developmental opportunities.

5

CONTAINING ADOLESCENCE IN ORGANISATIONS

This chapter continues the discussion in Chapter 4 about the impact of adolescent emotionality on adults with whom they are in contact. In this chapter the focus is on those who work with adolescents in professional capacities. The chapter takes a particular perspective, that of discussing how the power of adolescent emotionality affects professionals who work with adolescents, and thus provides a context of intensity to the work. As well as needing to contend with intense emotions, the professional can make use of these to inform work and understanding. The first part of the chapter focuses on some case examples of intense emotional contact with adolescents in institutions. These are then placed in the context of the changing nature of organisations, and the chapter ends with a discussion of how contact can be made with vulnerable adolescents who seek or need therapeutic help.

The emotional impact of adolescence

In Chapter 4, the example of Jamie and his parents illustrated the way that anxiety in and about adolescents can sweep powerfully through a family, and into organisations. In that example, the family, the school, the GP practice and the agency providing therapeutic work for adolescents were all impacted upon, to varying degrees, by the anxiety in and around Jamie. Thus relationships between adolescents and adults are subject to three particular forces – anxiety, the projection of some emotional states under the pressure of managing intense feelings, and being 'swept along' by adolescent emotionality. Understanding the impact of adolescence on groups, in families and elsewhere, and, vice versa, the impact of groups, families and organisations on adolescence, means taking these processes into account.

Case example: a pupil referral unit

Mrs J, a teacher in an educational unit for young people excluded from school (a pupil referral unit), returned to work after the Easter holidays to find that a group of her 16-year-old students blocked her way into school. They then ran ahead into the classroom and locked the door, leaving Mrs J standing helplessly outside. Feeling more dismayed than threatened by the boys' behaviour, Mrs J waited by the door, gathering her thoughts. She pictured an escalation of the difficulty if she had to seek help from colleagues, and she was also worried about what was being done to her classroom. Was some form of destructiveness taking place in there? Somewhat to her surprise the boys opened the door after a few minutes, and she was allowed to enter the classroom.

The students ignored her, and the contact she tried to make with them, as they moved wildly about the room and occasionally interspered their own rather manic conversations with some aggressive and offensive remarks about and to Mrs J. All her efforts to start the class working met with little response. Some students left the room, and others made a token gesture of acknowledging her authority before turning away from her.

By the end of the day, Mrs J left the school, feeling quite overwhelmed by powerful feelings of helplessness and despair. Among her overnight despairing thoughts were that she did not wish to return to the school, that she was a complete failure in her role, and that she had miserably failed these difficult young people she had been teaching for two terms.

There had been a holiday, and the students had been shut out from the school, the class and Mrs J's mind. It was also now the start of the last term at school for these boys, who were due to leave, and they were about to be permanently 'shut out' of the class and school. Two separations were in the air; the Easter holiday had just ended and the time for leaving school was approaching. The exclusion of the teacher, through locking the door, was an indication of how strong were these feelings about separation; how definitive and non-negotiable the experiences seemed to be. The effect was to push forcibly into Mrs J. a sense of the power of these reactions to separation and loss. The manic state of mind of the students suggests an attempt to overcome an underlying sense of depression and lack of control. Since these were adolescents who had been excluded from mainstream schooling, they were thus positioned as excluded, and inscribed with this status. The action they took had the quality of a resistance to what they had experienced – a taking up of a powerful role to reverse what they had been through.

Mrs J was subject to intense feelings of a desolate, despairing nature. She felt like leaving, and was full of a sense of failure, of being no good at her job. She allowed herself to be open to these feelings, and then felt overwhelmed by them, and isolated from colleagues. On the other hand, she did not simply react to the students, and tried to give herself time to think and find a way of responding which neither inflamed the situation nor avoided it:

> The next day she found a different scene. Some students were absent, and the others moved more listlessly and quietly about the school. When she entered the classroom, students were sitting quietly, mindlessly and without energy. They passively acquiesced with Mrs J.'s instructions, but none of them seemed capable of attempting even the easiest of tasks. Mrs J. actively engaged with them about their difficulties in learning, and one of them said he felt he did not know anything, and never would. Some of the boys drifted, again listlessly, towards the windows, and stood looking out of the class, into the school and beyond.

The students now seemed to resemble, in their states of mind, the despair and desolation Mrs J had felt the day before. The sense of failure Mrs J had felt was now located in the students, who now were listless, despairing and unable to work. The way the boys drifted to the windows and looked out reminds us of the locking out of Mrs J the previous day, but here the boys were once more recipients of an experience which, probably realistically, was quite foreboding. Exclusion from the mainstream appears embedded in this image, and the pain of facing the world beyond school, while feeling ill equipped, is evident. The boy who said, quite hopelessly, that he will never know anything plaintively expressed this.

Despair and failure appear to have been projected forcefully into Mrs J on the first day; on the second day, the students were more able to face these feelings in themselves, although this generated depression and listlessness rather than ho pe. The power and poignancy of this situation reflects the increasing emphasis on educational qualifications as a means of negotiating late adolescence. Therefore, a combination of powerlessness with anxiety about future vulnerabilities was especially acute in a context in which the power–knowledge connection was very much focused on, and institutionalised through, education. To leave school feeling that nothing is known, and no qualifications have been obtained, means also feeling that there is little or no agency available to oneself; no future.

Through not retaliating and allowing herself to experience these feelings and think about them – at some personal cost – Mrs J experienced powerfully the students' states of mind. It is notable that on being excluded from the class, Mrs J was able to wait, to try to think, and on being admitted to the class she aimed to make contact with the students, through continuing to try to work. These all constitute attempts to think and provide a reflective, containing space in these circumstances.

In working with adolescents in organisations and institutions, the impact of emotionality is likely to be extremely powerful, partly through the processes that develop in groups, and partly because of the level of disturbance, difficulty and damage in the adolescent population in these settings. This can be illustrated by work in an adolescent unit, where work is undertaken in the context of a high degree of suicidality and severe disturbance.

Case example: Sarah

Bowley (1996) discusses a suicidal adolescent, Sarah, 14, who repeatedly overdosed at times of separation or transition. One Christmas she refused to leave the in-patient unit, and when her foster mother arrived at the unit to collect her Sarah had disappeared. She later phoned to say she had taken an overdose. Since the unit was about to close for the Christmas period it was not possible for her to stay there, and staff were furious with Sarah, feeling their work and care for Sarah was being attacked. In fact only the nursing discipline were still on the ward at that point, the others having left for the Christmas break. The nurses were filled with murderousness towards Sarah. Sarah was in fact admitted to a paediatric ward for the break, and staff on this ward were furious with staff on the in-patient unit for abandoning Sarah at this time.

Rage, as a response to the impact of separation, spread like contagion through staff in the unit and then in the paediatric ward. Hinshelwood (1999) discusses distortions in individual identity in institutions and organisations in terms of contagion. 'Emotional states are coordinated across a group or crowd' who have something in common – 'a common internal object' – with which they all identify, to the extent that 'it is as if the individuals have suddenly contracted an infectious illness' (p. 155). In this case the staff, are 'infected' with violent rage and murderousness. It is easy to see the potential for inter-disciplinary and inter-agency fights breaking out as the meaning of these intense emotions splits these groups and distorts the meaning of the incident.

The powerful communication that ensued from Sarah's reluctance to move from the unit to the foster carer, and then her disappearance and her overdose, stir up terrific animosity and hatred, so that the accusation of abandoning Sarah runs through both institutions. The nurses feel abandoned by the other professionals in the unit and are then accused of abandonment by the paediatric unit. They are attacked with both sides of the same coin, so to speak. Thus the split and violent aspects of Sarah's inner world are projected into the staff, and mirrored there by the split between a child who is furious at feeling abandoned and a hospital which is furious about an 'abandoning' unit.

Sarah's background was very important both in understanding her suicidality and the particular impact it had on those involved in her life. She was physically abused as a baby, and through her early childhood. The staff in the unit found themselves very disturbed by the way they got to feel violently towards Sarah:

> In the in-patient unit, 'when we found we could feel the same level of violence towards her [as she had suffered herself] it was very disturbing. This would cause staff to overcompensate with Sarah for fear of acting on feelings of retaliation. It was difficult to show her anger or to stand up to her. Contact with Sarah was fraught with difficulty and she seemed to get under one's skin very quickly. For example, I asked how she was and she put on a phoney smile and said 'fine'; when I wondered aloud about how she really was she said, 'I'll throw you a fish if you like.' She made me feel like a seal, uselessly flapping my hands together. (Bowley 1996, p. 13)

The experience of being the recipient of cruelty as a baby and child pervaded Sarah's interactions, and at this point in her adolescence she was actively cruel in her interactions with others, though this involved using herself, and her body, as the target, provoking violent reactions in others. Her attacks on others included an episode where 'Sarah put some strong cleaning agent in the other adolescents' drinks unbeknown to them. One girl was very sick' (p. 13). This particular piece of cruelty projected into others the sickening quality of what Sarah felt she had had to take in herself in her abuse at the hands of others.

The staff, who were in receipt of these emotional communications from Sarah, felt themselves to be in projective identification with an abusing parent, or, through trying to compensate for this state of mind, they became passive. Ordinary attempts to make contact with Sarah led to her rejecting the help, and in the process making the staff feel useless and helpless, like seals. The attempts to keep hold of these feelings and thoughts through reflection enabled the workers to persist in the attempts to make emotional contact with Sarah, and understand her.

Being swept along with adolescence

The impact of these emotions on the staff makes for extremely difficult and demanding working experiences. Professionals contend with being filled up with intense emotions. In working with adolescents, there is a pull towards responding to the anxiety generated by becoming either passive or controlling. Organisations specialising in work with adolescents may develop specific institutional defences[1] against the impact of adolescence. In organisations where working with adolescence is part of the whole range of work, the organisational defences against the impact of adolescence may create a counter – culture, or alternatively affect the whole organisation.

Brenman Pick (1988), in discussing the emotional impact of work with adolescents in an analytic setting, focused on the intensity of the forces which are mobilised in the adolescent, and their impact on the worker. In adolescence, 'the power of the force by which the post-pubertal adolescent feels carried along by the impulses and defences he [sic] constructs against them' and in turn the adolescent has the potential to have this effect on the therapist. This leads to the adolescent trying to 'sweep the parents along with him, or angrily turn away and be swept along by the adolescent group' (p. 188). The therapist may be 'swept away' into 'colluding with his ideology or trying to sweep him away with a rival ideology' (p. 188). Brenman Pick compares two adolescents in analysis. The cases complement each other, for while 'John was carried away by the adolescent culture, Jane had the power to carry adults away with her' through a seductive superiority which aroused adults' envy (p. 189). John got 'drunk not only with alcohol and drugs but with his power to act out and have a good time'; Jane got the therapist 'drunk' on her seductiveness, and through projecting her sense of her superiority.

Thus both the therapist, or individual worker, and the organisation may develop a culture which coheres around an adolescent ideology (drunk on adolescence). These defensive cultures can include impulsiveness, rather than strategic thinking, individualisation of methods of work, relying on charismatic leaders, having grandiose or manic overestimation of the work. These defences may indicate that the organisation is vulnerable to the power of the forces of adolescence and become swept away with this power. Alternatively, the culture may cohere around an ideology which is an alternative to the adolescent's. Defences then have the aim of protecting the therapist from the fear of adolescent pain, especially the painfulness of change and separation. These defences aim to control the upsurge of adolescence. The 'forgotten' abjection of adolescence (Jacobs 1990) is felt to be threatening and to stir up fears of losing control of a more rational and balanced approach. Boundaries separating adolescents and adults in these circumstances may be strictly maintained, and the pain of adolescence is not felt consciously by the adults.

Defences against the fear of adolescent emotionality

Adolescents do have the capacity for reflection, and the increase in cognitive capacity through adolescence is an important developmental factor. Often, though, the intellectual capacities of adolescents, and their rationalism, can be used defensively to offset more abject aspects of themselves, and their vulnerabilities. A particular kind of problem develops when notions of adolescent rationality seduce the adults in organisations, into seeing rationality as the whole rather than a part of adolescent development. The importance of the adolescent's needs for adults to be available to receive projected anxieties, and to contain these, is then underestimated, or split off.

Case example: residential care

Watson and West (2001) discuss the impact of changes to the structure of residential care in a social services department. This account highlights the following features. The reorganisation created smaller units, located closer to the city centre from where the young people in care originate. 'Another reorganisation' is common in turbulent organisational contexts, and the anxieties about change were located between the workers and their managers. Because of the anxieties, a process of consultation was begun for the staff in which the consultants introduced the idea of obtaining the views of adolescents themselves. Staff felt powerless and that they had no control of the process of change. They were anxious about the future, and especially for their careers. They were anxious about running the units, and about having the skills that were necessary. The staff wanted reassurance from management that they were well thought of and needed. When feedback from the adolescents was discussed, it showed that they were accepting that the changes had been carefully considered, that on balance they were probably beneficial, and that it was worth 'giving it a go'. The adolescents agreed to pull together to make sure that things went as well as they could as long as the promised benefits accrued – namely greater contact with family and friends.

The adolescents were full of the spirit of interdependence and cooperation, resilience and flexibility, apparently unaffected by yet another change in their lives, while the staff were full of terror and trepidation. It seemed that some of the adolescents anxieties had been projected into the workers, increasing their anxieties and leaving the adolescents' free to be more rational. This picture of adolescent rationality and maturity does not fit with the realities of residential work with adolescents, who have usually experienced multiple disruptions in their lives, with damaging consequences for their development. They are likely to act out in impulsive and destructive or self-destructive and explosive ways. Alternatively they may be very defended against the pain of these experiences.

Mawson (1994) discusses how work with adolescents in residential settings is a powerful and intense experience. He emphasises the importance of maintaining a position which is neither unrealistically over-optimistic, nor overtaken by despair. This means being radically and deeply affected by the emotionality of the work. It is crucial, he concludes, that 'in painful and stressful work staff need to be given space to think about the anxieties stirred up by the work and the effects of these anxieties on them' (p. 73). Discussion of the anxieties makes it possible to retain a stance which steers a path between over-optimism and despair.

Over-optimism can take the form of 'empowering' adolescents, promoted by a belief in rationality and a philosophy of taking a positive approach, and splitting this off from the adolescent's intense needs of others. Beneath the application of this philosophy may lie a fear of setting boundaries, and thus being exposed to confrontation with the adolescents. As a result the adolescent' defences are encouraged and, without a reflective stance, workers are open to the projection of adolescent anxiety and disturbance. This leads to confusion of adolescent needs for containment, contact with others and intimacy, and the wish to be more independent in supporting themselves in gaining a greater sense of autonomy. The confusion of need, vulnerability and defences against the pain of being hurt in relationships with strivings for autonomy can be extremely disabling for both staff and adolescent, especially where the adolescent has experienced significant loss and deprivation.

Case example: Julia

Julia, a 15-year-old in a residential home, was very private to the point of excluding others from her thoughts and wishes. She had experienced a disrupted fostering and refused to contemplate a further placement. Thus she communicated that the pain of exclusion and rejection was so unbearable that she would not become involved again in an intimate relationship, in which there was the possibility of further experiences of this kind. Her workers experienced her as a rather unrewarding girl to relate to, as she invariably rebuffed attempts to get close to her. This could be understood as an expression of retaliation, making active what she had suffered passively from those in parental roles. Her perspective, however, was that she wished to have more independence and autonomy. Her residential workers became anxious about approaching her on many issues which were worrying, including her conflictual relationships with family members and difficulties in her relationships with peers and teachers at school. Occasionally Julia would reveal that she was worried, especially when a meeting with a family member was arranged, but it was very difficult to address these anxieties with her.

Julia found it difficult to acknowledge her need of others, and her wish for independence aimed to protect her from painful emotional contact. That Julia stirred up anxieties in others showed that she did have vulnerabilities and that she was not switched off from these feelings. Though she was felt to be immensely controlling, Julia also seemed fragile. The workers feared confrontation with her controlling defence, and were anxious about the potential explosiveness if Julia felt herself to be touched emotionally. This fear of breakdown in the adolescent was frightening to them. The workers tended to reassure themselves that supporting her wish for independence was a helpful way to proceed.

The risk of breakdown confronts the institutional defences of workers in these situations, who develop an optimistic view in order to contend with the extent of the pain and deprivation that they face in the adolescents they work with. The optimistic or positive approach thus becomes a way in which workers keep themselves going in the face of the kind of emotionality to which they are constantly exposed.

In Julia's case some consultative meetings with the workers focused on the difficulties of making emotional contact with her. This allowed the workers' underlying fears about Julia to be explored and discussed. Putting anxieties about her fragility into words provided the workers with a more reflective and flexible position from which to think about her, so that it was possible to separate out times when she felt a need for adults to take care of her and times when she was making more authentic bids for autonomy, rather than withdrawing defensively. This did not remove the difficulties, but it did provide the possibilities of greater emotional contact, and a sense of being able to think about ways of working with Julia.

Reflection provides the opportunity to put together splits which occur when working with disturbed adolescents. Focusing on disturbance without noticing possibilities for development, and focusing on development without noticing disturbance, constitute splits which can be constructed at the level of rival professional ideologies, and thus pull professionals apart.

Working with adolescents in turbulent organisations

Societal and organisational turbulence impact on organisations working with adolescence. Changes in organisations and the increasing speed of change add to uncertainty.[2] Repeated reorganisations can be obsessional attempts to control anxiety, uncertainty and ambiguity. Professionals working with adolescents have to contend with a kind of mirroring, in that changes from the outside have a similar structure and effect to the emotional impact of adolescence on the adult. Cooper (2000) suggests that the loss of certainties of tradition creates a problem of mourning, which is complicated because of the lack of a sense of definition of the new. In the turbulence of recent changes, organisations are significantly concerned with negotiating loss, and with issues of control and the fear of loss of control. In organisations there are conflicting ideologies, characterised by Cooper (2000), in the context of changes in welfare as a whole, as the replacement of a 'logic of compassion and development' by a 'logic of control and inspection'. The relationship which is based on a link to emotional experience is abandoned (p. 124), and this threatens the possibilities of providing reflective, containing spaces.

Bell (2000) gives an example where a cruel, omnipotent organisation is perceived to blame staff for all mistakes, creating a culture of blame and punishment. Thus in the event of mistakes the omnipotent organisation 'would hold staff completely responsible and ensure they were punished' (Bell 2000 p. 35). Bell discusses the impact of a suicide of an adolescent in a residential unit: 'At the first meeting after a suicide had taken place, the staff were understandably stunned, especially as the patient was not thought to be in much immediate danger.' However, organisational stresses had preoccupied the staff who then began to feel guilty that they had neglected to discuss the patients: 'Soon there emerged the idea that if we had talked about the patient we would have saved her life' (p. 35). This became a pervasive sense that suicide was everywhere: 'I suddenly found myself wanting to use the meeting to talk about any patient under my care who was suicidal. I then remembered that it is often the patient whom one is not particularly worried about who actually commits suicide. So the category "suicidal" widened its reference until it included all the patients under my care' (p. 35).

Of course the suicide of a young person is an extremely difficult experience, which can test judgement and which is extremely painful. Balanced judgements are more difficult to attain in turbulent organisations, where the external social changes mirror the impact of adolescence on the professional, and where anxiety is high because of the pervasive anxiety. Morale may also be affected, leading to a stance which is easily overtaken by despair. The capacity to hold professional judgement and to manage risk means, however, that assessments need to be made on the basis that risks exist. Uncertainty and anxiety is part of professional judgement-making, and in turbulent organisations decision-making takes place on a ground which is in motion, not from a centred, solid, unmoving certainty.

Reflection on adolescent emotionality in a psycho-social space

Making sense of the impact of adolescent emotionality on professionals requires space to think, to discuss the impact of these emotions, and to use this kind of discussion to understand meaning. Through this process it is possible to get to know something of the quality of the adolescent's projections. The examples in this chapter illustrate the way that adolescent emotionality impacts on the professional, and the potential for understanding the adolescent which is obtained from reflecting on these experiences. This applies the ideas about countertransference that were developed by Heimann, in which the analyst has the means for

> comparing the feelings roused in himself [*sic*] with the content of the patient's associations and the qualities of his mood and behaviour, [and thus] for checking whether he has understood or failed to understand his patient. (1960 p. 10)

The aim is to 'sustain ... feelings as opposed to discharging them'. Brenman Pick's idea that adults get swept along with adolescent emotionality and ideology is a specific application of this theory to adolescence. In a reflective, containing space, discussion aims to understand the feelings raised in the therapist or professional worker through the impact of contact with adolescence. A process of differentiation – which emotion is coming from whom, or where? – takes place alongside an acknowledgement of the multiple or plural layers of meaning, involving simultaneously the adolescent and the organisation in its context. The reflective space for thinking about adolescence takes on the qualities of a psycho-social space if the context of adolescence and the context of the worker are taken into account. Thus discussion about anxieties raised in the course of work can be self-reflective of the organisation's work through including reflection on the meaning of adolescence that is attributed in specific contexts.

Making contact with adolescents in turbulent organisations and contexts

Contemporary therapeutic services for adolescents are concerned about the difficulties of making and maintaining contact with groups of vulnerable young people. Adolescent attendance at therapeutic services is notoriously irregular. Young adolescents do not often self-refer, and many adolescents drop out of therapy prematurely. Since difficulties in adolescence tend not to be resolved with the passage of time, and difficulties at adolescence are thus likely to persist into adulthood, in a form at least as severe if not more so severe, the problem of attrition rates is a serious one. 'One suspects that those who drop out are often those in greatest need' (Mak-Pearce 2001 p. 15). Making contact with adolescents in a way which sustains possibilities for therapeutic help a major issue for organisations offering therapeutic services to adolescents. The new diverse contexts of adolescence and the changing nature of organisations present both risks and threats and possibilities for these services. A number of recent suggestions have been made about the way therapeutic services should focus on maintaining contact with vulnerable adolescents.

Mak-Pearce (2001) argues for a rapid response for adolescent requests for therapeutic help, and a methodology of focusing on the future transference:

> The future transference is a term I use for the current feelings about how the relationship with the therapist will be at some point in the future. To my mind it is the key to engagement ... What kind of figure will the therapist be? How potent, how useless, how intimate, how loved, how hated will the therapist be? (p. 19)

This approach creates a focus for the reflective stance of the therapist. Other suggestions about ways of making contact include the following:

- Offering a number of modalities of engagement, including face-to-face therapeutic consultation, and completing questionnaires in the therapy setting. The use of questionnaires can augment the process of making contact with adolescents (Radonic 2001) and of understanding their relationships with others. Radonic reports on successful contact with an adolescent who appears to be not psychologically minded.
- Actively providing information about the aims and objectives of therapeutic consultation, so that these can be discussed.
- Structuring the interview to take responsibility for the direction of the session, and not to leave the adolescent in silence. Questioning which shows an interest in the adolescent and the adolescent's preoccupations may facilitate a sense of feeling listened to (Baruch 2001).
- Supporting a vulnerable adolescent's attempts to attend therapy by arranging for an adult to bring them to sessions until they can manage this on their own.

- Structuring sessions on a regular, weekly basis, and providing possibilities of a number of meetings, in order that the adolescent can get used to the therapeutic process.
- Involving the adolescent in the process of referral, even when the referral is made by others who are worried about the adolescent (Anderson and Dartington, 1998 p. 4).

Positioning adolescents as negotiable, and negotiating with them, and so providing choice wherever possible, are important ways of bridging the power relations between adolescents and adults. Sometimes the adolescent needs a space made for her/him in the midst of everything that is going on around her/him through a direct invitation to a consultation. Other adolescents need to have the adults in their network get together to contain their anxiety about them before a therapeutic consultation is offered to the adolescent. This is particularly important with vulnerable adolescents, particularly those in care and who have a wide network of adults involved with them. Consultations with networks contain the anxieties about adolescents and either provide the professionals, carers and parents with a more reflective basis for thinking about the adolescent or else allow the adolescent to feel able to emerge from within the anxieties and concerns of the networks and claim space for her/himself. Some adolescents need encouraging into contact and others need to be left with space to choose to make contact. Some need informal contacts in the community, through professionals skilled in this kind of informal work, while others need to be given the space and privacy of an appointment in a clinic setting, perhaps at some geographical and emotional distance from the home and community. Some need the reassurance of meeting someone who is felt to be the same, and others need to move into a context of difference.

All of this suggests plurality and the need for multidisciplinarity in meeting the challenge of making contact with vulnerable adolescents. Noam's case, Rosa, was quoted in Chapter 3 to illustrate the need for flexibly allowing adolescents to experience belonging in 'contexts of affirmation'. Some vulnerable adolescents make a link with a therapeutic organisation and despite not attending, or missing appointments, clearly have the therapist and therapy in mind. Sometimes effective work takes place through the existence of this kind of link! While acknowledging difference and plurality, and trying to provide flexibility, are important in engaging adolescence, thinking about the best approach to each adolescent needs to be undertaken within a framework or ideology which offers a rigorous approach to reflective thinking about the emotional contact with the adolescent and its meaning. A usual structure of weekly meetings, which are time-limited, provides the framework for the therapist to maintain a reflective space, which is crucial for the understanding of the multiple levels of meaning that emerge in work with adolescents.

There are many ways in which adolescents make contact, and these demand internal flexibility both in therapists and in organisations. Attrition forms a prominent anxiety in contemporary work that is connected with the need to reach adolescents who find it difficult to use therapeutic organisations. However, the principle of making emotional contact is an important focus of work with all adolescents, and the principles are the same: detailed reflective work and discussion by the therapist; attempts to understand the meaning for the adolescent; and struggles to find ways of communicating about the adolescent's emotional states and their impact on the worker. This involves considering deep anxieties. A case example may illustrate some of the vicissitudes of this kind of work; it addressing a particular anxiety, namely the silent adolescent.

Case example: Daniel

Daniel was 14 when he first came to therapy. After his first session I came away with a strong feeling of not liking him, which, after a struggle, I let myself think might mean that he had a sense of not liking himself. In the second session this was exactly what he told me – he didn't like himself. He was brought up, as I have said, by a young single mother, and had very little contact with his father. Recently his father had written to say that he would like to make contact and Daniel was trying to work out how to respond. He did not know how to get hold of the – probable – mixture of excitement, resentment, anxiety, pain and wish for revenge which was churning inside him. Moreover, as he was clearly getting a sense of himself as probably gay, the invitation to meet father held poignancy in terms of his developing sexual awareness of himself.

Daniel had no difficulty coming for his therapy, but he was almost completely silent in the sessions. It was not a silence that led me to think he was about to walk out and never return, but rather one which was extremely awkward, and which gave me a feeling of being really quite unable to speak to him. I felt extremely perturbed by this very restrictive context, and I began to feel a sense of dread when it was time for his session. Daniel arrived very early for his sessions, sometimes over an hour early. He sat in the corner of the waiting room under the care of the receptionist, who perhaps could have been seen by him as a 'mother in an apron'. He came reluctantly from the waiting room, as if the therapy session had interrupted his quiet sojourn there. So, despite being so early in the building, he was often late for his session. I sometimes felt I might 'forget' to call him, to leave him uninterrupted, and I experienced both a sense of relief at the thought of not having to face him and also a sense of guilt about wishing to avoid him.

At some point, I realised that the situation mirrored Daniel's dilemma in the external world. Should he leave the comfort of mother to meet father? Should he leave the waiting room to see his male therapist? I knew I could not interpret along these lines; it would be not only indigestible but a cruel penetration of him. His father's letter was felt to be an intrusion and he resented it, but for father not to write would have been worse. I now began to feel the silences as a wish for and a fear of penetration. If I spoke I was penetrative; if I was silent I didn't care. But still what eluded me was a way of trying to communicate some of these thoughts in a way which would be containing, rather than inflammatory. I felt I was in a position with no room to move, no choice. In the silences of the session I began to feel something competitive, seductive and ruthless, focused on a decision about who leads, who penetrates whom.

In some consternation I discussed with colleagues what to do. Daniel had said that he struggled to put things into words, and one suggestion made to me was that I should offer him some drawing materials. My first reaction to this was that it would have an effect not dissimilar to a lead balloon, and I feared Daniel would see this as me patronising him by treating him as a smaller child. On further thought I wondered if there might be some merit in the idea. I decided to try it. I obtained the materials – some pens and a notepad – and discussed it with him. I said that I had wondered if instead of feeling that he had to always speak to communicate to me, he might like to write or draw. He was noncommittal, neutral, but not objecting. I said I would think about it some more and I would then decide what to do. The next week I said to Daniel that, as he could see, I had decided to put some pens and paper on the table for him to use, if he wished.

Daniel did not use the pens and paper, but he did begin to talk to me. At first he would wait for a prompt from me, but eventually he began to take the initiative. The feeling in me, in which there seemed to be nothing between intrusive penetration and passivity, was also transformed, and many of the issues that had been unspeakable were opened for discussion. He did not use the pens and paper – but then he did not write to father. It only occurred to me later that I had presented him with a mirror of his dilemma – did he want to write or not? Somehow, he felt that he had been given choice, but there was a deep sense of loss too, a decision that he would not write.

The struggle to make contact with Daniel illustrates the process of working within a reflective space, in an organisation and in contexts of difference and turbulence, and the way that Daniel made use of the organisation and the therapist within it. The process of reflection on feelings and meanings within a structure or framework underpins thinking about adolescence, and can be applied, flexibly, to different adolescents in different contexts.

Summary

- Relationships between adolescents and adults, in the latters' role as professionals in organisations, are subject to anxiety, the projection of intense emotions, and these can be disturbing.
- Containment of intense adolescent projections is provided by thinking about the meaning of the emotional experiences workers are 'subject to', rather than being 'swept along' by adolescent emotionality. The intense experiences workers are subject to may or may not be held in the structures of the organisation. The emotional impact of adolescent emotionality, especially in the very disturbed adolescents in residential care, can affect staff across institutions and between groups in organisations, creating professional conflicts.
- Defences against the impact of adolescence range between control and passivity. Splits between adolescent rationality and potential for development, on the one side, and focusing

on disturbance and not noticing developmental possibilities, on the other side, are also typical defences used in working with adolescence.

- Organisations, in the current social context, are turbulent through involvement in processes of rapid change. Professionals working with adolescents have to relate to a subject – adolescence on the move – from within organisations which are also in flux.
- In the context of change and turbulence, making therapeutic contact with adolescence is a priority. These processes are complex, and require, in general terms, the capacity to respond flexibly, while maintaining a rigorous framework for thinking. The need for reflective space to think about the work is paramount.

6

ADOLESCENTS AS TEMPORARY OUTSIDERS: DRUGS, OFFENDING AND ANTISOCIAL BEHAVIOUR

Dartington (1994) has proposed that taking up a position of 'temporary outsidership' is a necessary part of adolescent development, and that it provides a way of assimilating the transition from being a child in the family to being an adult in the social world. This chapter discusses difficulties in adolescence from the perspective of outsidership. The concept of temporary outsidership is explained and applied to issues in adolescent development, leading to a focus on the anxieties and difficulties in maintaining a position on the boundary, between the inside of the family and the outside of the social world. Failure to reach and sustain the position of temporary outsidership leads to distinctive adolescent difficulties. Some of the difficulties which may be thought of as characteristic of adolescents as outsiders, especially antisocial behaviour, offending behaviour and drug use, are discussed.

Temporary outsidership

The idea of the 'outsider' originates in a modernist discourse, derived from notions of the 'outsider' as rebel, philosopher or seer. It is an idea which has a number of applications and meanings. The idea of the outsider is developed from thinking about groups:

> The outsider is one who is part of a social group but who, for a variety of reasons, takes a position on the fringe or the edge of the group . . . The outsider is one who is part of a social group but who, for a variety of reasons, takes a position on the fringe or the edge of that group. The role of the outsider must be clearly distinguished from the outcast. The outsider is of the group and definitely performs some function *for* the group. Of course he or she may become an outcast, but only if he or she becomes too much of a threat to the cohesion, structure and belief system of that group. (Dartington 1994, pp. 91–2)

The outsider is also necessary for the group in providing a capacity to observe the group, though this may be welcomed or felt to be persecutory. The outsider is likely to have to endure rejection. Dartington quotes from Camus's *The Outsider* who 'drifts in the margin, in the suburb of private, solitary, sensual life'. Thus:

> The outsider is well placed to observe the world. The marginal position is a potentially creative one because the intellectual and emotional distance from familiar experience makes it a space for a new viewpoint or an original thought to take place. (p. 92)

Dartington argues that the adolescent needs to take up a position of 'temporary outsidership' in order to develop a scepticism towards the rules, attitudes and beliefs of the group – the family group in this case. Thus the outsider is concerned both with a quest for truth and authenticity and with thinking thoughts based on experience. The position of temporary outsider aims to learn from experience rather than to take as read the inheritance of other's thoughts.

The outsider has a difficult position to maintain, since particular emotional and cognitive capacities are required in order to sustain the quest for truth and originality. In particular, there is a precondition that the adolescent has a sense of finding some solitude and aloneness rewarding, rather than being persecuting and therefore lonely. This depends on the internalisation of good experiences, and the presence within of a coherent and cohesive sense of self (Stern 1985). Becoming an outsider may be driven by a number of experiences or internal configurations. It is easy to confuse this constructive or creative withdrawal, in order to be alone with one's own thoughts, with a retreat from the difficulties in relationships, which may constitute a retreat from relating.

The position of outsider can be developed quite concretely in adolescent group life. Socially, it is a feature of adolescence, usually most evident in those who are often referred to as 'mid adolescents', that an outsider position is adopted through congregating around telephone boxes, garage forecourts, outside a shop or in some other specific vantage point. Adults witnessing this divide into those who fetch in the police to move the teenagers on before there is trouble and those who lament the lack of facilities for adolescents. Philanthropic efforts then lead to the construction of a café, or, in a more commercially exploitative mode, a 'teen disco'. But the café remains empty or the teenagers attending a teen disco stay outside for most of the evening!

In truth this is a partial analysis. Accounts of the teen disco provide a compelling reading of the varieties of adolescent outsider relating. The teen disco trades on the wish to be grown up and to imitate the over-18s. Over-18s are barred. Staying outside is associated with wishing to take alcohol, which is not allowed inside the disco.

An account in the London *Evening Standard*, under the heading 'Homework, hip hop and hot pants', highlights that inside the disco there is a sense of merger in the same sex group: 'The cloakroom is a rail of identical denim jackets. "Don't lose your ticket," the frantic-looking cloakroom lady is saying'. Maybe she can be thought of as being the recipient of projected anxieties about the loss of individual identity, for which the cloakroom ticket is in fact a return ticket to individuality. The same story explains the reversed use of the word 'boo' to mean good, not bad, as in the phrase 'Wicked, I got a lot of boos.' One participant, a teen DJ, on the other hand, retains his sense of his position as an adult-in-waiting, and thus his individuality, and his sense of his position 'on the boundary'. He retains a connection between being a 'kid', a child to his parents, and having adult aspirations, being separate and being a DJ. He says 'I want to be an adult. I'm going to be an adult for the rest of my life, but I can never be a kid again.' At this juncture his mobile phone rings and he hears his father is waiting round the corner to collect him. His phone rings again and he answers 'Hello mum – see I am a kid'.

In teaching groups of professionals working with adolescents, the idea of the outsider resonates with personal recollections of adolescence, or current contact with adolescents. One teenage memory told in this context is of sitting on a wall, with friends, across the road from her home. From here the friends could monitor every movement in their own and each other's homes and discuss their and each other's families. Looking into parental homes was presumably accompanied by a wide range of thoughts and phantasies.

In early adolescence, exploring the inside of one's own family and in particular the minds and attributes of parents can be a difficult and inhibiting experience. By late adolescence, a narrative about one's parents is an essential aspect of identity. This process may be accelerated by exposure to change and loss in the family, forcing the adolescent to think about aspects of her/his parents s/he would sooner not yet know. The capacity to know another's mind depends on the ability to develop and maintain a sense of separateness from the other, and the experience of separateness may prove to be difficult to manage, raising anxiety.

Adolescents may take up these rather concrete positions of temporary outsidership with some difficulty, relying on the group and projecting ambivalent feelings into adults. There is a sense of strength through solidarity in the group which covers anxiety and fragility in the individual. A parent described her daughter and her friends, in their early teens, gathering in the entrance hall of her house. She had to walk round them for some time, as they stood there in a kind of indeterminate state in which the passage of time seemed to play no part. She found herself oscillating between passivity on the one hand, leaving the adolescents to whatever they were doing, while being aware of them, in their gathered state, or she would become filled up with a sense of wanting to say 'For heaven's sake, make your mind up; either come in or go out!' The adolescent is much more able to maintain a position at some distance from the inside of the family, and to contemplate the social world outside when in a group, than when alone. In this positioning a projection can nudge adults to take up passive or controlling positions in return. Uncertainty, ambiguity, ambivalence and guilt may all be involved in these projections.

In this sense the outsider position, is formed from a spatial image, in which there is movement to occupy a position on the boundary. It is a position which is inevitably anxious. On the boundary, the anxieties may be of a kind consistent with sitting on the fence or more tortuously – sitting astride barbed wire. Because the outsider position in adolescence stirs up anxiety, there exists the likelihood that anxiety will be projected into others, but also there are opportunities for the adolescent to test the ways in which s/he can draw on internal experiences of containment in order to tolerate anxiety. The experience of outsidership thus holds the possibility for the adolescent of getting to know about anxiety, risk and limits. Strengths and limitations may become known, and thus the adolescent uses the position of temporary outsidership to augment identity, and a sense of being oneself, in one's own body and mind.

Potentially, there are multiple experiences of outsidership, as the adolescent makes the transition from child in the family to adulthood. In particular, there are three ways in which the experience of temporary outsidership opens up a potential or transitional space.[1] These can be summarised as:

- *Space to feel one's own emotions and to differentiate them from others.* If outsidership is a tolerable experience, anxieties may be engaged with. If it is not tolerable, anxieties may need to be repudiated, denied or avoided. The adolescent may oscillate, perhaps intensely, between moments in which the outsider position is taken up and those when it is repudiated. At the extreme, subjectivity may become fixed or frozen on either side of the boundary of the temporary outsider position.
- *Space within relationships which permits some freedom of movement.* If the adolescent experiences the potential contact with others in the outsider position as introducing a gap between self and others, a process of becoming separate is begun, of which increasingly complex possibilities in relating to self and others are the consequences. If the gap and

complexities pose threats which cannot be tolerated then there are defences against difference by attempts to restore sameness, to merge or destructively to break links with others. There may be omnipotent attempts to fix relationships and the sense of self-relating to others through the use of drugs, sex, or adhesively maintaining contact rather than permitting separateness.

- *Space within the self for flexibly developing different aspects of the self, in love, friendship, intellectual, artistic and cultural connectedness.* If the 'outsider' experiences the self as having new opportunities, and anxiety can be tolerated, possibilities are opened for increased awareness of different aspects of the self, which may be fragile or perhaps uncoordinated. If there is too much anxiety, or terror, from the plurality of these experiences, and the notion of internal division that is driven into awareness, catastrophic fears of inner fragmentation are stirred up, so that defences against this fear are generated, in varying degrees of control, violence and mindlessness.

The concept of temporary outsidership is best represented as providing space for thought, awareness, creativity and increasing complexity. These are possible if there is fluidity of movement across the boundary, rather than getting 'stuck' or frozen on the inside or outside, or at the threshold. Britton's thinking about the container–contained relationship, as discussed in Chapter 1, showed that the two elements of sanctuary and meaning required a capacity to be 'inside' as well as 'outside'. His patient Miss A was paralysed at the 'threshold' because of the claustrophobia of the inside and the dangers of the outside. In attachment theory, the capacity for exploration is dependent on a secure base. The adolescent who is fluidly able to move between both subject positions – outside and inside – retains the possibility of reaching into the family, or outside into the wider social world for exploration.

Failure to reach the position of temporary outsider

In contrast to the positioning of those adolescents who can tolerate experiences of temporary outsidership, there are those adolescents and their families who cannot tolerate the in-between states which require both attachment to a secure base and a capacity for exploration.[2] In her account of the temporary outsider, Dartington provides examples of families who fail to attain a boundary position. In these families there is a sense of either being locked into a closed world or being pulled apart in a kind of centrifugal process. In Chapter 4, the closed dyad of Simone and her father is an example of being 'stuck' on the inside.

The consequences of the intolerance of temporary outsider-ship can be severe. For Dartington, the meaning of this 'right in or right out' mentality is that the wish to separate is synony-mous with hatred, which may not be survived, and which may lead to a catastrophe. This has some congruence with Blos's views that if the process of separation is not sustained then adolescents may try to replace the emotional work of separat-ing through concrete actions, imposing geographical distance between themselves and parents. Alternatively, through suc-cumbing to regression the adolescent will be taken over by a longing for a return to childhood unity, or an idealisation of the state of being on the inside.

Adolescent difficulties may be related to the problem of maintaining a position of 'temporary outsidership'. It is one of the functions of therapeutic work with adolescence to provide, literally, a space outside the family and other social networks, which is, however, through the content of the therapeutic discussions, not cut off from either of these. Thus the psycho-social space of therapeutic consultation occupies a boundary position.

Establishing the boundary position means the adolescent has the capacity to move backwards and forwards – to progress and regress, to seek nurture and develop relationships within the family – and yet be free enough to move outwards and experi-ment, try things out in the wider social world, and get back again. Once a 'temporary outsider' position is maintained the adolescent can begin to exert some active control over infor-mation flow, and to have opportunities for maintaining some selectivity about what parents and family get told. Similarly, not everything within the family need reach the world of social rela-tionships outside it. One emblem of adolescence – the diary –

indicates the capacity of the adolescent to reach a position on the boundary, where all need not be said, and much of what is said can be contained by oneself, with the help of the diary. On the other hand, breaches in the 'secrecy' of the diary, or its adjunct, the address book, can be thought of as indicating a leak in the adolescent's 'adolescent' persona.

Adolescent problems and the temporary outsider position

Getting stuck on one side of the temporary outsider boundary is indicative of the kind of problem an adolescent is having. Some adolescent difficulties relate to being stuck on the inside – for example school phobia, being the victim of bullying, eating disorders. Other problems, especially acting-out sexually, antisocial behaviour, such as delinquency and criminality, becoming immersed in drug cultures and gang behaviour, are more indicative of being stuck on the outside. This is, though, a crude distinction. It is more helpful to think of outside 'stuckness' as indicating a position with regard to difficulties experienced in intimacy and the need for others, and disowning a sense of one's own vulnerability. The inside stuckness has the meaning of being unable to separate, or move away from the position of childhood dependency, or finding within oneself the means to undertake the work of separation. This chapter will discuss adolescents stuck on the outside and in Chapter 7 there is a discussion of those who are stuck on the inside.

Stuck on the outside

Adolescents who appear to break links with adults and families are in various ways left stuck on the outside, without recourse to a return to emotional connectedness with parents. Blos (1967) describes the stuck outsider: 'in his actual separateness and independence he experiences an intoxicating sense of triumph over his past and slowly becomes addicted to his state of apparent liberation' (p. 82). This forms a starting-point for a discussion of delinquency, and of drug-taking. Adolescents may be pushed into these through being in painful predicaments with parents.

Case example: George

George, 17, hesitantly telephoned to ask for a therapeutic consultation. Between this phone call and his appointment, he and a friend broke into a shop. George said that he had second thoughts after his phone call and he had not intended to keep the appointment, but that now he was very worried about what he had done, and he feared being caught. George told me his father had left the family when he was 13, and, though there was a mystery about why he left, George thought he was in trouble with the police. I was struck by the timing of the break-in, between referral and appointment, and also that there seemed to be a connection, through offending, between George and his father. George said he had no premeditated plan to do the burglary, and he still did not know why he did it. He thus seemed to be 'subject to' intense internal forces of which he knew very little.

Freud (1916) wrote about criminals from a sense of guilt, whose actions indicate they acted upon expression of an intolerable sense of guilt internally, to which the subject had no direct access. Breaking and entering may be considered as an expression of being forcibly kept out from, together with a wish to gain access to, and thus control from within, an unavailable object. The burglary seemed to represent George's fury at being abandoned and a rather self-destructive identification with father. Another example is of a teenager who was 'looked after'.

Case example: Terry

Terry had been looked after since he was seven. His mother was not at all available to him, and he spent four years in a foster home. This disrupted when he was 11, and then he spent some time living with relatives, in foster care and in residential homes. Each placement ended when the relative or carer felt that Terry had become too demanding or too difficult. At critical times in these placements Terry would either leave, go missing, or get involved in a violent episode, either within the home in which he was staying at the time, or in school. These events tipped the balance against him, and he was excluded. Terry was contributing actively to worsen his situation, which reached the point that he was not taken in either physically or emotionally by anyone. When he was 15 a new social worker made a determined attempt to find him a more enduring and meaningful environment and she worked hard with him, the network and within her own agency to achieve this. When she found a placement for him that would take care of him and provide education, Terry went missing, and was later found sitting outside a house, which he had broken into.

Terry's break-in, and the fact he waited to be caught, seemed to vividly convey his feelings about his relationship between himself and others. Not only was he an outsider, and requiring others to find him somewhere to belong, but the relationships involved breaking and entry. This seemed to vividly express his sense of permanent exclusion, outsidership turned outcast. The only kind of relationship in which there could be a transition between outside and inside, for Terry and George, necessitated a violent mode of entry. The experience of absent, dead, unavailable, neglecting or abusing parents provides an almost impossible task for adolescents in mourning these losses and maintaining a sense of integrity, identity and development. George's situation provides further illustration:

George's father's departure left him with a mother whose mental health was fragile. She suffered recurring periods of intense depression, and sometimes took an overdose. George was painfully involved with his mother's illness and propensity to self-harm. He was worried about his mother and worried by her, feeling very exposed to her behaviour and responsible for her. He hated being in the home, and occasionally found ways of escaping – to play on a friend's computer or to watch his football team. He felt unable to concentrate on his own life. He did not take GCSEs, and this left him extremely frustrated and ashamed, feeling that he had let himself down. He felt bitterly that he had more potential than this. He half-heartedly tried to find work, but could not feel free enough to engage in the process of finding a job. Several times he started to get work and then did not follow this through. His fragility was such that when he was in his therapy he was quite genuinely shocked if I showed I had remembered things he had said to me. He told me he thought this remarkable, that he did not think people did this. This had the effect of stirring up within him complex, intense and ambivalent feelings about what he had lost and his current predicament.

Being stuck outside, not having parents who were able to attend to his developmental needs and to keep him in mind left George feeling preoccupied with his parents, worried about his mother and pained and angry with both parents. These preoccupations filled his mind to the exclusion of a capacity within himself to maintain a focus on his own life. His tentative move to ask for therapy was an attempt to find some space for himself and it caused a backlash within him, which led to his offending before his first appointment. Being in therapy meant contending with considerable turbulence within himself.

Delinquency, antisocial behaviour and outsidership

The adolescent's delinquency and deviance is part of an inheritance of traditional ideas about adolescent conflict, turbulence and rebelliousness. It is the aspect of adolescence which gets adolescence hated and from which folk devils (Cohen 1973) arise. Blos (1967) saw the upsurge of violence as internal and inevitable, owing to the increase in instinctual tension and the loosening of infantile ties to the parents. Some acting-out is therefore to be expected, and it constitutes a 'holding position until progressive development is rekindled again' (p. 82). But if acting-out becomes excessive or prolonged it indicates a 'an attempt to escape from an overwhelming, regressive pull to infantile dependencies, grandiosities and gratifications' and thus 'the adolescent who runs away, drives off in a stolen car, leaves school, 'bums' his [sic] way to nowhere, takes to promiscuity and to drugs' is 'resorting to emergency measures' and attempting to accomplish internal separation by external means.

Bowlby, Winnicott and Erikson took a slightly different approach to delinquency, emphasising the impact of the environment in a more concrete form. Deprivation is the cause of delinquency. The delinquent 'was not to be regarded as feckless, bad or evil, but as an individual seeking to rectify that which did not feel right inside' (Wilson 1996, p. 395). Thus, in the face of depriving experiences, there was a note of protest in the delinquent act, 'as something positive, self-affirming and, above all, hopeful for the individual' (p. 395). In certain circumstances, delinquency has meaning and affirms authenticity, through its paradoxical 'doing wrong, it carries with it an unswerving sense of rightness' (p. 394). Though Winnicott's writing on adolescence is often accepting of the unacceptable (Perret-Catipovic and Ladame 1998) the connection between meaning of the delinquent act and the background of deprivation and disruption fits the examples of George and Terry. Thus it is the extreme rupture or trauma that breaks up the identity of these adolescents, so that the impact of the environment is to render the adolescent a more or less permanent outsider, whose delinquency, or 'anti-social tendency' as Winnicott called it, 'is a reminder of a hurt or disturbance brought about by environmental failure' (Wilson 1996, p. 395). The adolescent's delinquency is a form of resistance, within power relations.

On the other hand, the remorselessness and imperiousness of delinquency cannot be separated from hating and/or envying others, who possess something that the adolescent desires and wishes to possess. This puts stealing and violence in the same field, in which the adolescent aims to take, inauthentically, from a competitor or to wipe out the competition, internally or externally.

Anderson (1997) takes a view about violence which has a point of contact with Blos. 'Putting the boot in', or apparently mindless violence, is a response to the overwhelming feelings that are stirred up in some young people on encountering depressive anxieties. Feelings of vulnerability and dependency, concern for the other and being separate are repudiated, located in a recipient through projective identification and then attacked. The recipient can be another person or an internal, vulnerable part of the self, or both simultaneously. The problem is therefore the essential fragility of the individual, which cannot bear depressive anxieties.

Attention to the delinquent act suggests multiple meanings. For example, Waddell (1998, p. 139) shows that stealing – in the case of her patient, Christine, who stole from her family – can represent

- restoring a lost relationship, rather than mourning the loss and accepting separation;
- depriving someone else of their possessions (and it may thus be located in revived Oedipal conflicts, especially a jealous attack on the same-sex parent;

- feelings of guilt which desire punishment (as in the examples of George and Terry), and an avoidance attacks on the self by a jealous parent;
- depriving another through envy and rage;
- a response to change and loss within the self.

Thus 'stealing is one of the most common manifestations of "acting out" [in adolescence]' (Waddell 1998, p. 139).

The relationship between trauma and damage, acting-out and the capacity to make contact with, and to some extent bear, depressive anxieties is central to understanding these young people. Rustin (2000), in discussing two young adolescents placed for adoption, shows that manic defences, 'excitement powered by hilarity and obscenity [hold] anxiety at bay quite effectively', and these two siblings clung together to relieve 'potential loneliness and the terror of facing so many worries about themselves and their future' (p. 80). The two, Lorraine, 14, and David, 10, seen together, played noisily, and

> 'They squabbled, snatched and chattered abusively. David was full of dirty talk and kept up a torrent of verbal abuse of Lorraine and she retaliated by hitting his head.' Rustin comments that she felt she 'had two very wild toddlers in the room, in overgrown bodies'. (p. 78)

The question that is then raised is how far either or both of these abused and disturbed adolescents have the potential to make emotional contact and how far each can tolerate their vulner-abilities. How far, it may be asked, can they leave the manic 'pro-tection' of the group-become-gang? Or, alternatively, how much will the hate, rage and envy lead to an obliteration of the desire for contact, so that a defence against contact prevents access to other people's minds in an empathic way, and delinquency or violence becomes a 'career' or a fixed subject position?

When vulnerabilities cannot be tolerated individually, a group may provide a way of sticking together to provide a sense of strength against powerful perpetrators of painful experiences, and functions through projecting vulnerability into a chosen target, within the group or outside. The gang 'turns their passive suffering into active cruelty' (Waddell 1998) through identification of this 'target' who is then placed in receipt of aggression and murderousness. Bullying occurs when there is a reciprocal fit between the projection of murderousness into someone identified as vulnerable and the victim of bullying projecting aggression into the aggressor. The gang need not be an actual group. In Rustin's example it is a sibling pair; and it is possible in these dynamic terms to see some use of drugs in this way.

Case example: Jill

Jill, 16, was in foster care and her relationship with her foster carers had become tenuous. She was developing a wild lifestyle of clubs, promiscuity and drug-taking. She had a wide circle of friends, and she moved between them so that she was able always to be in contact with someone else. When friends or boyfriends were not available she had a mobile phone to which she was completely attached, and if this failed she could get drugs from a dealer she knew. Although, given these aspects of herself, it may seem unlikely, Jill came to her therapy, and she did have a capacity to make emotional contact, together with some awareness of the meaning of her manic defences. The end of her therapy sessions became a point of crisis for her, and she seemed to feel intensely a need to fill the gap or void between herself and therapy immediately. This drove her to action. One form of this was to make phone calls on her mobile before leaving the room. More extremely, she went straight from her therapy to buy drugs. At these times Jill would not be aware of the causative impact of separation, but rather would talk about being unaccountably upset, or preoccupied with therapy being 'difficult', in order to try to make the overwhelming quality of her emotions more manageable.

Despite the fragility of Jill's subjectivity, she was able to bear emotional contact, and indeed longed for it, but this stirred up overwhelming feelings of loss and pain, which had to be kept under control. Feelings of vulnerability were unwanted and hated, and humiliating for her, but paradoxically she needed to feel some vulnerability in order to be able to be in contact with herself and others. Success for Jill was being 'cool', but when she achieved the desired 'cool' this also meant that she had split off her needs and vulnerabilities so that she was at risk of damaging herself, and her relationships. It was through getting into distressing and distressed states after something went amiss in one of these relationships that she felt a need for help, and this state of mind, her more vulnerable sense of herself, returned her to her therapy.

Drugs and subjectivity

The use of drugs is a complex subject. Social analysis asserts that pressure on adolescents to use drugs, alongside the development of a 'lifestyle', constitutes both a pressure on young people to take part in consumption, to develop a lifestyle, and also that it is an aspect of resistance. For example:

> In a moment where most young people can 'manage' little else, the body provides one important site for management and also becomes the primary vehicle for the achievement of pleasure ... The use of drugs ... And the cultivation of a particular fashion for oneself can, in this context, all be seen as attempts to stake out an independence from the parental and societal regulation of these bodies. (Pini 1997 p. 163)

This analysis, which owes much to Foucault, sits alongside an older view in which adults are hypocritical; they castigate the use of drugs but use their own, especially alcohol and nicotine. Van Heeswyk (1997), from a psychoanalytic view, proposes the idea of 'benign addiction' in which alteration of perception, through 'coffee, beer or heroin' changes how we feel. The hopeless problem before the use of drugs becomes easier in the 'benign addiction' paradigm. 'It may still be hopeless, but it is no longer serious' (p. 65). Clearly this approach is medicalised, especially in the treatment of depression, anxiety and ADHD (Attention Deficit Hyperactivity Disorder).

Bollas (1991) takes a different view, in which he asserts that 'hallucinating from ingestion of a drug is an act of violence against one's subjectivity' (p. 146). Writing specifically about 'tripping' Bollas points out that the alteration of mind through tripping is not the same as dreaming, since the drug usurps the function of the ego in processing 'lived experience'. The taking of a drug is a 'casual almost serene moment', in which the pill is 'dropped' like an atom bomb 'dropped' from a plane. The analogy of violence casually done places the taking of (some) drugs in a contemporary social context.

Between these positional aspects lies individual meaning. Jill took drugs because she was a member of a group of teenagers who were in that kind of scene. She also took them at particular points in time, primarily to express her fury at the fact that separation from others is a necessary and unavoidable experience in life, and she wished to avoid the overwhelming feelings that she experienced when she felt vulnerable. She also did it as a form of casual violence against herself and her objects, which was self-destructive (this was in fact her judgement of herself) and she took drugs because she had to endure awful experiences inside herself that resulted from the abusiveness and deprivations of her past. The use of drugs, then, has multiple meanings in adolescence. It can indicate a group identity, a process of exploration, or a problematic and pathological situation. Rodriguez de la Sierra (2000) has proposed that alongside sociological explanations of drug use – peer group influence, experimentation and rebellion against adult values:

> the use of drugs in adolescence is closely connected with failed attempts to deal with intense aggressive and sexual feelings, which the adolescent then tries to relieve by turning to pills or injections that bring deceptive tranquillity to his or her troubled mind. (p. 78)

The relationship between the adolescent drug user and the social world can be masochistic, and also, omnipotent in seeking magical solutions to experiences of separation and loss. The same person may be involved with drugs for all these reasons.

The task of therapy, with Jill, was the rather awesome one of trying to find ways in which she could feel more able to bear her own emotions. This meant developing a sense of choice rather than compulsion, tolerating emotional contact with others, even though it meant at some points separating from them; managing to be alone, being 'inside', belonging, rather than fated to be an outsider, giving up, or relying less extensively and exclusively on manic, omnipotent and masochistic defences and relationships as a response to pain, frustration and separation. This, once more, constituted a process of becoming 'subject of' rather than 'subject to' internal experiences in a given social context, or, in Williams's (1998) phrase, giving up dependency on an 'unreliable container'.

Summary

- 'Temporary outsider' is a term which describes the adolescent in developmental motion, an in-between state, on the boundary between the family and the social world. It can be experienced in different ways as adolescents make the transition through from childhood towards adulthood.
- There is a hopeful, 'becoming' aspect of this if adolescents can tolerate the experience of a gap between themselves and others. Widening and deepening of relationships, awareness of self and a sense of power and capability are made possible by temporary outsidership, and the flexibility of moving between inside and outside in a fluid way.
- If the anxieties of the boundary position of temporary outsidership are too great, the adolescent may get 'stuck' on one side of the boundary – inside or outside, with consequent problems in development.
- The problems of being stuck on the outside include antisocial behaviour, delinquency, and drug-taking and acting-out. These are linked by an intolerance of experiences of separation and depressive feelings and the stirring up of violent and manic defences against pain. From different theoretical perspectives, there are multiple meanings for each kind of behaviour in different contexts.
- The case examples show that when emotional contact with others and a sense of belonging within intimate relationships are precarious, defences are mobilised against the turbulence aroused by intimate contact with others. Acting-out is a means of expressing, resisting or obliterating the pain involved.

ADOLESCENTS WITH DIFFICULTIES IN ACHIEVING SEPARATENESS

Many adolescent difficulties relate to not being able to tolerate the 'gap' between self and other upon which subjectivity is founded. Being stuck on the inside means that the impact of internal, familial and social factors, often in inextricable combinations, slows down or brings to a halt the adolescent development towards separateness and relative independence of parental figures. Thus, either physically or emotionally or both, the adolescent is unable to become a temporary outsider. In order to explore the psycho-social aspects of these difficulties in adolescence, this chapter will discuss adolescents with phobias, eating disorders and disabilities.

Not separating

The negotiation of separation, as demanding internal work, akin to mourning, can be replaced by an imperative demand on others to provide separateness and independence as though it is a gift. This was stated very vividly by a 15-year-old adolescent:

Case example: Colin

Colin, who was in fact a very small boy, in appearance much more like a 10-year-old than a boy of his age, had a difficulty with eating, and with growing. He felt trapped in his smallness, weighing under six stones

(38 kg), not eating and worrying that he was losing friends. At the same time he said 'There is a bit of me that is happy to be like this. It is like being in a cell with a heavy door that will take ten years to open. And I can't find the box with the rusty nail in it. I need to spit it out.' Colin felt trapped and faced with an immense labour to achieve more openness under his own efforts. His hopelessness led him to give up and ask for others to do it for him. He implored me to 'tell them [his parents] to give him his independence'.

He could not contemplate or conceptualise undertaking himself, in conjunction with someone else, such as myself in role as his therapist, the emotional work that would bring about a negotiation of independence with others, over time. In his metaphor the rusty nail in the box seemed to have a deathly constellation, invoking a coffin. He felt that anything that took a long time meant things got worse. This also applied to therapy:

> He said 'There's no point coming here for a long time. Either you'll give me an idea that works or not. The longer you go somewhere the less helpful things get.' At first he told me there were no problems in his family, but then he said that his mother was ill, and there had been deaths in the family. He was worried his mother would die. When we spoke about the difficulty of feeling someone was leaving him, or he was leaving someone, he said, 'It is difficult, it's like a death.'

When separation is equated with death, the difficulty of separating becomes very frightening. Phobic defences get mobilised. The combination of parental illness and an intruding sense of death invaded Colin, so that he was stuck on the inside. Interestingly, he told me that he never drank milk, and he had been told that he had refused milk from the time he was weaned from the breast. The failure to mourn and accept substitutes went very deep in his relationship with his mother, with whom he could be thought to be over-involved, so that there was a fusion between them, with Colin being ill because his mother was ill.

Flynn (2000) discusses how different insider and outsider defences in young male adolescents – delinquent, phobic, obsessional and psychotic – all shared a 'continuously overly involved relationship with the mother . . . based on incestuous patterns' (p. 62). One such adolescent:

steered his way into his early adolescent experience very slowly and gradually by reluctantly relinquishing his latency pursuits and preoccupations. These included maddeningly abstruse games and procedures he would devise, and ways of talking and thinking that could be shared with practically noone but his mother, who seemed to be the sole initiate in Brian's one person cult. (p. 62)

The wish for, or even requirement, of a special relationship with mother can leave young adolescent boys unable to tolerate separateness, and seemingly arrogantly or contemptuously tossing aside relationships with others.

Case example: Jeremy

One boy, Jeremy, 14, could not bear to be the same as other boys, and his eccentricities – seriousness, 'nerd'-like refusal to join groups – were extremely provocative to his peers, particularly as he had great difficulties with his aggression, and projected it into others. He became extremely disliked by peers, which reversed his sense of feeling extremely disliked by his parents, who had not been satisfied with one child and had two more, his younger brothers. Being disliked by his peers brought a kind of satisfaction for him, and he was at times unmercifully bullied. 'Look', he seemed to be saying while taking himself hostage, 'at what this eviction from the special relationship does to me'. Desperately disillusioned, he felt that any closeness with others brought betrayal.

With Jeremy, there was no space on the boundary; he was right in or right out. His expectation of others was that they would have him and only him or they were history. Being separate and sharing others' affections were unthinkable propositions. Dartington's view of the outsider was that when outsidership was felt to be impossible, it was linked with 'an unconscious conviction that the wish to separate is synonymous with hatred, that, in families, the reserves of love will not survive this hatred, and that family catastrophe will ensue' (p. 94). Phobic states are one defence against this fear of catastrophe.

Case example: Sally

Sally, 13, refused to go to school. She had been involved in an incident at school in which it seemed that another girl had criticised her, and since then she had absolutely refused to leave the home unless her mother was in constant attendance. Sally came to therapy with her mother and older brother, Sean, who was 17. Sally dressed more like a smaller child than an adolescent, and she seemed completely overwhelmed by her mother, who was insistent that she must be seen by therapists who were parents. Sally's mother was adamant that if the therapist was not a parent then she could not possibly understand her. Eventually, Sean, taking the role of family historian, helpfully told us that there was another child, a girl, who had died in infancy. Both Sean and Sally were in fact terribly guilty that their own hostility and murderousness to this baby had somehow contributed to her death. Sean was ostracised for talking about this baby, as the family never spoke about it.

The indigestible, unmournable loss of this baby was a powerful unspoken presence in this family. Mother's insistence that Sally should be seen by therapists who were parents projected into the therapists the feeling that she had ceased to be a parent to her baby. Moreover, if Sally grew more separate then she would lose her too. Sally's role was to remain close to mother, and not separate.

Williams (2001) has written about the disorganising effects of silence surrounding a loss, and particularly a death of a baby, when these are projected into another child in the family. Sally was in more difficulty than Sean because her place in the family – the last surviving baby – attracted more projections from mother. She was impelled not to leave her. The equation of separateness with death, or catastrophe, leaves the adolescent unable to reach temporary outsidership, because fear of the outside is produced through the projections of an aggressive nature onto the outside. The phobic and bullied states of mind converge. In Colin's case, the feeling of having something deathly, or deadly, inside him prohibited the exploration of the inside space, and thus the outside world, and growth towards the boundary and separating, through projection, was invested as dangerous.

Disability in adolescence

Adolescents who are disabled get 'stuck on the inside' within a context in which physical separation and autonomy is perhaps restricted. Primarily, the experience is of facing difference – not being like others – within a context of negative attributions:

> Most of the people we have dealings with, including our most intimate relationships, are not like us. It is therefore very difficult for us to recog-

nise and challenge the values and judgements that are applied to us and our lives. Our ideas about disability and about ourselves are generally formed by those who are not disabled. (French and Swain 1997)

Organised by society as 'docile bodies' (Foucault 1977), disabled adolescents constantly face experiences of difference or separation, especially through educational segregation. Special schooling can be excluding, or it may provide opportunities of experiencing similarity, in a kind of diaspora: 'It [special school] was a liberating experience. It taught me how to like myself, to take pride in myself, and most of all to be sensitive to the needs of others' (French and Swain 1997, p. 201).

Trevatt (2001) discusses how thinking about disability is a 'dangerous area to express views in', and how muddled the thinking of adults can become between notions of normality and the limitations of disability. The idea that a disabled adolescent may have the same interests, desires and illusions as other adolescents is countered immediately by a differentiating process within the adult, as if to make decisions about what aspiration and desire a disabled adolescent may have or may not have. Thus adults fall between ideas of nurture and growth, and of managing illness, disability and limitation.

Interestingly, Miller (1998), when working psychotherapeutically with learning disabled adolescents, found that the experience of sameness and difference had a powerful impact in the therapy. She describes Beth, a 16-year-old with Down's syndrome, with a severe learning disability, and who lived in a children's home. Beth caused many difficulties for the staff of this home, especially when she imitated other adolescents' aggressive behaviour in a contagious way. Beth's history was one of frequent disruption to continuous relationships, beginning when she was placed in foster care as a one-month baby, perhaps, or probably, because her parents were unable to face the fact of her disability. Miller describes the first therapeutic consultation with Beth, in which three professionals were present:

> When I suggested Beth might like to draw, she suddenly began to participate very actively in the session, drawing food and telling [us] to do the same, handing out paper and pens. She drew attention to ways in which we were the same; we all had black shoes for example. (p. 43)

Milller comments that the defence against painful difference could have been the focus of intervention, but if, imaginatively, the therapist tried to think about Beth's state of mind, there is a relief and freedom from thinking that 'we are all the same'. In a later session, the idea of difference disrupted Beth's contribution, until she could find another contact of sameness. Miller then discusses the implications for identity;

> When the [learning-disabled adolescent] talks it is not clear to whom he or she is referring – to him or herself or the therapist – the direction is reversible. This mode of communication seems to lie somewhere between the concrete and the symbolic; there is meaning, but it is difficult to ascertain to what or to whom it can be attributed. It is as if there is a potential two-person relationship but the identities of subject and object are not clearly located. (p. 43)

The effects of the interaction between disability and experiences in the social world are extremely entangled. Beth had a deprived, abusive and disruptive background in terms of her relationships, and the problems in identity cannot be separated from these or the limitations imposed by her disability itself. The problem arising from the phenomenology that Miller describes is that social experiences, which are internalised, complicate differentiation of self from other. Beth is looking inside for contexts of sameness. When she has a notion of sameness with another she can relate, play and creatively communicate.

Thoughts and feelings about the relationship between body and mind may become subject to multiple meanings. David, 18, who had been born without arms from below the elbow, and who had a foot amputated in childhood, designated his disabilities as 'his bits missing'. Williams (1997), who discusses this case, describes how David had 'bits missing' in his childhood. His teenage mother and her family were not able or willing to care for David continuously, so that, in the absence also of a father he had never met, David spent time in children's homes. He had poignant memories of the frequent separations from his mother, which conveyed his wish to hang on to her as she left. Unable to do this with his arms, he focused on her with his eyes instead.

David's response to his predicament was to overcome it, and he did make himself very 'able' through physical activities and painting. Williams felt that 'I was asked, for a long time, to pretend that the disability and the many "bits missing" in his body and in his life did not exist, or if they existed, that they did not matter' (p. 80).

Trevatt discusses the tensions for physically disabled adolescents who have fantasies for the future which are probably illusory and which can be painful for adults to bear, and difficult for them to challenge. He refers to young people who 'seem to live more in a fantasy world to the extent that they need me to believe that their fantasies are true' (p. 100). The strength of these fantasies are linked with anxieties about loss and death, reflecting a painful reality that some young people will have severe limitations in terms of their independence and autonomy, while others face an early death or a very uncertain future life expectancy. Williams reports David moving between two states of mind, one in which there was a sense of real achievement in which emotional contact was possible, and another in which he was swept away in phantasies of an omnipotent nature. In these moments it was difficult to make emotional contact, and David seemed 'extremely elusive. He could probably only tell me about the pain of not being able to take a firm grip on his object by evoking this feeling in me' (p. 80). David used his eyes to compensate for not being able to make a grip on another in other ways. His eyes fixed on other people, and he only began to be able to let go of this rigid grip when he internalised containment of his anxieties. This included both an appreciation of his real achievements and awareness of the quality of his omnipotent phantasies. Williams formulates the transition from the necessity of the emotional need of another in the external world to relying on an internal world separate from others, in parenting roles, as requiring the 'internalisation, or at least the beginning of the internalisation, of a reliable internal object' (p. 88).

Eating disorders in adolescence

Eating disorders have been thought about as evidencing a difficulty in the adolescent of accepting a developing sense of adulthood, and as a defensive reaction to emerging adulthood and sexuality (Plaut and Hutchinson 1986). The low body weight of the anorexic girl, and her loss of periods, maintain a childlike bodily state and a rejection of the bodily world of adults. Williams (1997) points out that anorexic girls are 'often terrified of sexuality in general, but terrified of penetration in particular' (p. 118). To remain looking like a child means not facing the process of adolescent development and the world of adulthood, with its separateness and sexuality.

Eating disorders are complex, however, and 'loom large as potent metaphors of our times' (Williams and Bendelow 1998 p. 75) Giddens (1991) suggests that 'anorexia represents a striving for security in a world of plural, but ambiguous objects. The tightly controlled body is an emblem of a safe existence in an open social environment' (p. 107). The risks of engagement are not felt to be worth taking, since a loss of sense of self-worth is experienced through engagement. Giddens quotes the title of Sours's (1981) book, *Starving to Death in a Sea Of Objects*, in this context. Bulimia and obesity present different images and ways of attending to the same dilemma – safety through control in a plural, ambiguous social world. 'While bulimia represents the unstable double bind of consumer capitalism, anorexia (i.e. the work ethic in absolute control) and obesity (consumerism in control) embody an attempted resolution of cultural contradictions' (Williams and Bendelow 1998 p. 75). These analyses of eating disorders include the idea that there is a tremendous asceticism in the trials, punishment and purgations that are done to the body, through which arises a sense of achievement, which overcomes despair, and which through control acts on the wish for self-denial and of being an active agent. The validity of the methods and outcomes may be questioned from a psychoanalytic viewpoint, where the central problem – relating to others – is evaded by these compulsive and often increasingly and intensively cyclical defensive manoeuvres. Where Giddens talks of empowerment in this context, it has to be questioned whether the empowerment is real, illusory or simply defensive. On the other hand, the accounts provide a way of understanding the social and cultural pressures which affect adolescents, in particular the problems of plurality and risk seem especially pertinent; subjectivity is avoided through eating disorders.

Social and cultural analysis of eating disorders emphasises the gender divide. It is a mainly female phenomenon – or, it can be said, girls and women 'pay the greatest material and symbolic toll' (Williams and Bendelow 1998 p. 75). The gendered nature of eating disorders is connected in these accounts with the obsession with exercise and body-building in the 'asceticism' of eating disorders. Many more adolescent girls experience eating disorders than boys, but boys too have eating disorders – and are increasingly noticed as such clinically.

However, it is argued that there are particular, gender-specific pressures that bear on adolescent girls. On the one hand the emphasis on thinness and the devaluation of women through negative societal images create a context in which adolescent girls may become ambivalent about their development of women; much of this discourse centres on the body. On the other hand, girls are socialised differently from boys, and their relationships with their mothers are more tense, more divided and including a more specific tension with regard to identifying with their mothers (Sayers 1991, Bordo 1993); under such pressure one solution may be to remain as an insider and not to venture into the world of adulthood.

In that there has recently been a recognition of young male eating disorder, this may reflect some changes in the constitution of masculinity. Sayers (1991) characterises female adolescence as divided in relationships, male adolescence as divided internally. For males to experience eating disorders there is a prerequisite, in this analysis, that they are torn internally, with ambivalence in relationships and fear of loss of control, rather than being split off from emotionality.

Psychoanalytic thinking has recently extended the understanding of the internal dynamics in eating disorders. Magagna (2000) argues that anorexia means not simply closing the mouth to food, but also closing the mind to emotional experiences, which means also withdrawing from the world of others and particularly the nurturing possibilities in relationships. Williams (1997) has described a 'no entry syndrome', in which the anorexic adolescent closes down the possibility of taking something in. This forms a defensive system, in which the fear of taking in is experienced by the adolescent as so acute that it becomes a dread. If the anorexic teenager feels something has to be taken in, then the impact of this is akin to a breaking and entering. Forced feeding thus breaks through the defensive system and simply reinforces the dread and sense of persecution; the emotional resistance to taking in is in this way reinforced. It is important in this sense to think about the parallel meaning of physical and emotional digestion (Briggs 1995). The anorexic is not made better by putting on weight; in fact 'emotional anorexia' continues to dominate, in some cases, the mental life of the anorexic even after an increase in weight and an improvement in eating patterns. Instead of bursting through this defensive system, Williams advocates noticing and talking about the defence, being receptive to what the adolescent can take in (being prepared to use teaspoons rather than tablespoons, so to speak), while at the same time maintaining vigilance with regard to the fluctuations in weight (weighing is usually undertaken by a professional other than the therapist, and this establishes a couple working with the adolescent).

The bulimic teenager presents a similar picture; emotional bulimia can exist alongside physical bulimia, in patterns of gorging or bingeing followed by evacuation. For example, one teenager bought clothes which she wore once and stuffed into her wardrobe, then periodically cleared out the wardrobe, putting the clothes into plastic bags and throwing them away.

These accounts suggest that there is something in particular taking place in the minds or internal relationships of anorexic and bulimic adolescents. Williams argues that the eating-disordered adolescent has experienced a particular quality of relationship with her parents, usually the mother, in which she has been the receptacle for undigested emotional experiences of the parent. That is, instead of the parent being a container for the adolescent, the roles have been reversed. She gives an example of a teenager, Sally, whose nightmare was being invaded through every orifice by tadpoles. This constitutes not only a fear of sexuality (tadpoles being recognisable as sper-matozoa) but 'a more pervasive dread of allowing anything to come inside . . . every orifice is a possible access to persecutors' (p. 120). Thus, though it is often the case that adolescents with eating disorders have had difficult and painful life experiences

– some having suffered sexually abuse and/or other traumas – eating disorders are underpinned by a problem in the arena of containment, which affects internalisation, or taking in from others.

A complementary approach which however emphasises much more the aims and motives of the eating-disordered adolescent's inner world emphasises the attacks on life (Magagna 2000) and the hidden – but active – murderousness (Lawrence 2001). Lawrence in fact uses this analysis to demonstrate the internal difference between the bulimic and the anorexic. Both the anorexic and the bulimic patient have a paramount need to control the other. In particular, the problem which needs to be controlled is a sense of life and liveliness in others, which excludes the patient, and the prototype for this experience is the parental couple (Britton 1989), whose fertility is evidenced by the existence of the patient. Since this experience of another's life and liveliness is totally unbearable and unimaginable, the eating-disordered patient tries to destroy liveliness, both through the impact of the eating disorder on her interpersonal relationship and in her own inner world. The anorexic needs to render her 'object' helpless, and thus to have to observe her destructiveness. A distinctive case of anorexia in a teenager illustrates many of the above points.

Anorexia

Case example: Samantha

Samantha, a 16-year-old, came to therapy on the recommendation of her teachers, who were concerned about her. Sam's parents died in a road traffic accident when she was nine. This had been an intolerable and indigestible emotional experience (Williams 1998) and Sam never talked about her parents. Avoiding contact with this, she 'got on with her life' and in particular concentrated on her schoolwork, where she had developed a reputation for extremely diligent work, and she had high expectations of herself. Her teachers said that she was increasingly difficult, she lacked concentration, and her work was very inconsistent.

It was very striking in her therapy that Sam had great difficulty in taking in from me. She would contest things I said, making a great deal of minor discrepancies and quibbles, so that the point of any interpretation was lost. Soon, she became very preoccupied with a wish to stop coming, and in each session would raise the idea that I should let her not continue. I had the feeling that it was important to resist this, but that it was also important to try to find a way of thinking about it with her, and that was a very delicate thing to do. My sense was that she presented me with a 'no entry' system of defences as discussed by Williams, and that beneath this was a powerful murderousness, which she was not really aware of. It also seemed clear to me that the discussion about stopping therapy was in some way connected with the loss of her parents, and that she was not consciously aware of her feelings about her parents, or, indeed her murderousness.

Eventually, though I had to wait a long time, she told me she had problems with eating. She told me she had begun to have difficulties with eating in her early adolescence – though no one knew, and she described herself at this point as bulimic, keeping her difficulties hidden by eating and then vomiting. In telling me this she talked also about her parents' deaths, including many details of her feelings at the time and afterwards.

Instead of this bringing relief and improvement, Samantha's wish to face her difficulties and her past brought about a terrible struggle with her internal demons. She became seriously anorexic, in the grip of a terrible internal murder, which meant I had to face the feeling – and at times the prospect – of losing my patient in an awful way. I felt condemned to watch her, helplessly, just as she had helplessly suffered the loss of her parents.

That her parents' deaths were felt by her to be a very cruel experience seemed to be evident from the way she treated her therapy, making active what she had previously suffered passively, and putting both of us through a life-and-death struggle. In this example, there is a tremendous power of enactment, in which the eating disorder, in a highly suicidal form, impacted upon me in a way which made me feel extremely helpless. It seemed to be the only way she could work through the indigestibility that had become frozen inside her. Eventually, however, her murderous attacks on herself and her objects relented and she was able to relinquish her deadly grip on herself, and others, and begin to turn towards life and development. Finally she left for university, leaving her therapy at the same time, and effecting a fundamental aspect of adolescent development – being able to leave parent figures, rather than being left by them.

Bulimia

The bulimic, more secretively than the anorexic, tries to conceal her destructiveness from the object. However it is control which is paramount: the ultimate form of control is effected through an underlying phantasy of murder. The anorexic wipes out in her mind the existence of others, and then, through turning things on their head, in a perverse way, the wiped-out and objectless world is idealised. Lawrence provides the example of a patient who dreamed that she was having intercourse with her boyfriend when suddenly everything went white and the boyfriend was no longer there; the patient said how much she loved white. It is thus murderousness which makes active the impact of anorexia which is usually transmitted to others as passive. Murderousness towards the self actively places the anorexic in a life-threatening as well as a self-damaging arena; there are also links between this kind of material and suicidal dynamics (see Chapter 8). The anorexic is caught between two opposing trends, one on the side of life and the other favouring death rather than growth. 'Both the life-seeking and the death-seeking factors are writ large. This "fierce dispute betwixt damnation and impassioned clay"' (Williams 1978) has the adolescent trapped at the threshold, and, in long-term eating disorders, addicted to the state of near death.

The bulimic's vomiting represents a phantasy of killing internal objects, but the bulimic has less of a stranglehold on the object than the anorexic and the objects keep coming back to life, only to need killing off again. The bulimic needs to be a serial murderer. Lawrence illustrates through a bulimic patient who was unable to read before her analysis, but, when she felt able to do so, read only books on serial murder. This is then linked with Klein's (1935) thinking about the manic defence which is employed to control dangerous internal objects, and in particular to keep at a distance feelings of concern and compassion for the object. In some cases, even noticing the separateness of the object as another human being can trigger the defences of the eating disorder. Thus the eating-disordered patient gets involved in 'activity which to the external observer seems pointless. This often includes intense physical activity, but also the massive and unnecessary scholastic over-achievement found in many young anorexics' (p. 51). Though writing on the whole about adult patients, Lawrence also links her thinking about eating disorders with the adolescent issue which revolves around the place which is given in the adolescent's world for relationships with others, and what has been called the 'omnipotent quest' of adolescence (Greenberg 1975).

Case example: Carol

Carol's descriptions of eating were characteristic of a bulimic teenage girl, bingeing on ice cream which she would take for herself from the fridge. She said, for example, she would eat three ice creams – but it could be anything that was there. Then something seemed to take over and it would become mechanical. She would keep eating and afterwards she would vomit.

Carol was worried about not being liked or popular at school and she thought popularity was in indirect proportion to her weight. When I saw her she was a small teenager of 15, whose shape was somewhat hidden by a bulky jumper. She told me she weighed just under 8 stones (51 kg) at present, though her weight fluctuated and she had recently been 10 stones (61 kg). She thought that her bulimia had been an 'ideal solution' to her problems. By vomiting she was able to eat, and not gain weight, thus satisfying her craving without losing her popularity. She felt 'cheated' that, when her weight fell as she continually vomited, she lost her periods.

Carol's 'ideal solution' was seen in the way she continually bypassed emotional as well as physical processes. She avoided problematic feelings in her relationships with others, particularly her parents; and aimed also to 'bypass' the therapeutic process. Indeed any process involving taking in was to be treated in the same way, including learning at school. Bulimic interactions pervaded her world, including her view of her parents' behaviour. Carol wished to play down and evacuate her difficulties, to which she felt her parents overreacted:

She was worried that she upset her parents, and she just wanted to be rid of the problem. She added that she wanted 'a form of therapy that

will soon be over'. Carol spent time in my room greedily feasting on the
objects in the room. Especially she would stare at the books.

I felt I was under considerable pressure to collude with her,
especially to spare her from commitment and contact. Instead
of thinking with her about her states of mind, she seemed to
want me to let her raid my bookshelves, take away a book and
return it when she was ready. This I learned reversed her experiences with her parents from when she was very young. Both
parents worked and Carol would let herself into the home after
school, and prepare her own meals from food in the fridge.
In Carol's life, people were turned into fridges, and this was how
I felt in working with her. The fridge could be raided at will,
whereas the communications with me were restricted-to-face to
face meetings at specified time intervals. The fridge was an in-
animate, cold-storage object, but one which permitted access
under her control. Live contact was thus controlled and deval-
ued, at the tyranny of an infantile part of her which could not
bear to depend on someone who was separate from her. The
experience of separation was short-circuited and avoided
because it was intolerable and stirred up powerful feelings of
being out of control. Carol was someone who could not bear the
thought of therapy more often than once a week because it
meant that the increased frequency provided not more help but
rather more experiences of separation. She needed to be right
inside, or right outside, and the position on the boundary, tolerating separateness and accepting a limit to the control exerted
over others, was too anxious for her.

Carol's pervasive bulimic state of mind, in which evacuation
– churning out – was predominant exemplified issues of control
and the need for a short cut through emotionality and relationships. This led to problems of subjectivity and objectivity. The
lack of a perspective, of what is serious, is absent or changed
into a kind of curiosity about how something works, while the
'I' is restricted. On the other side of this 'short cut' was a fear
of overwhelming feelings, especially depression and distress,
which became unbounded, in an enormous sense of loss and
damage.

Carol binged and then became depressed. She was worried
about the loss of her period and felt it might be lost forever, in

which she communicated a sense of never being able to grow up and become a woman. She felt she had 'messed herself up' (an image of being covered in her own vomit). Fleetingly and elusively in these moments of this state of mind, there were possibilities of making emotional contact. In these moments it was possible for thoughtfulness to be present. Painfulness could be digested, in other words, with thought.

Summary

- The adolescent who is 'stuck on the inside' has disconnected from the adolescent process, and development towards adulthood has reached an impasse. These adolescents cannot bear to be separated from external parental figures (including therapists), and the task of relinquishing a hold on an external figure is felt to be terrifying.
- The clearest examples of adolescents who get stuck on the inside are those where there is a social refusal, such as school phobia. In these situations the external world becomes invested with extreme dangerousness, where the fear of separation is closely connected with a fear of death. Actual, unmourned losses may play a significant role.
- There is an extremely entangled and complex interaction between social, physical and emotional aspects in the development of insider difficulties. In some situations, negative experiences emanating from the social world may be extremely important; in others experiences of deprivation, disruption and loss in childhood may powerfully affect development.
- Transition from reliance on an external to an internal parental figure in stressful psycho-social contexts requires the internalisation of reliable, containing parental figures.
- Fear of loss of control, and the need to control the separateness and independence of others, are significant factors in the development of eating disorders. The eating-disordered adolescent attempts, through the use of the body, to arrest development into adulthood.
- Eating disorders, which are emblematic of contemporary adolescent difficulties, are complex in that there is both a wish

to retain a childlike relationship with parents and also a wish to break links with dependency upon others. Thus in eating disorders there is not simply an insider wish to stay a child, but also a hatred of dependency and the emotionality of contact with others in relationships. The 'attacks on life' form an extremely important aspect of the self-destructive and at times suicidal eating-disordered adolescent.

8

PSYCHOTIC AND SUICIDAL STATES IN ADOLESCENCE

In this chapter the extremities of adolescent difficulties are discussed, especially suicide and suicidality, and psychosis and psychotic anxieties. The psycho-social context is discussed in order to consider the intersubjective as well as the subjective contexts of becoming suicidal or psychotic subjects in adolescence.

Psychotic subjects

Novels such as Kafka's *The Trial* and Eco's *Foucault's Pendulum* describe a psychotic world, in which the internal becomes located in the external or social world, a feature of psychotic subjectivity. According to Kennedy (1998):

> In psychotic states, the elements of the subject are felt acutely to be 'subject to' outside forces. Instead of being part of the subjective organisation, the social field is then experienced as outside the subject, and often then the place where projections are located. (pp. 188–9)

However, the processes of projection from inner to outer are reversible in contemporary social contexts, so that a fragmented and dangerous external world is introjected and internalised. In the contemporary social world, the breakdown of expectancy and continuity has been described as destabilising and unstable. The social world impacts through the proliferation of images, and the breakdown of gaps between time and place, which is immediate, sudden, global and virtual. These images are also invasive – 'space invaders' – so that 'our reality is transformed and made flimsy by its penetration by invading images ... chaos, flimsiness and instability [is] our experience of reality itself' (Lash 1990 pp. 14–15). The way the internal world is formed from the cultural context may be inferred from the way psychoanalytic descriptions of the internal world are taken from external phenomena. Rosenfeld's (1987) discussion of the 'mafia gang' and discussions of internal hostage-takers and terrorists come to mind.

It is the boundary between two spheres – conscious and unconscious – which is subject to erosion. Bion (1962) described this as the 'contact-barrier', through which the unconscious and conscious domains are kept distinct:

> The contact-barrier is therefore responsible for the preservation of the distinction between conscious and unconscious for its inception ... the contact-barrier permits a relationship and preservation of belief in it as an event in actuality, subject to the laws of nature, without having that view submerged by emotions and phantasies originating endo-psychically. Reciprocally it preserves emotions with endo-psychic origin from being overwhelmed by the realistic view. (pp. 26–7)

The contact barrier, in other words, creates balance while preserving the distinctiveness of difference. Adolescents, subject to internal change and social repositioning at the same time, are particularly vulnerable to the breakdown of the order of unconscious and conscious, or primary and secondary process.

Case example: Judith

Judith, who was not psychotic, but was subject to intense psychotic and depressive anxieties, illustrates the confusion of internal and external through the actions of powerful projective identification.

Judith was extremely sensitive to pain, and she reacted strongly to any sense of being 'touched', in which she would become verbally very defensive. She told me of a memory of early childhood when she felt furious with her cat for scratching her. She was not just hurt, but mortified, so that physical pain and outrage were both present. In murderous retaliation she shut the cat in a cupboard. She felt better for a time and then realised she needed to release the cat from its confinement, as she began to feel responsible and guilty for its imprisonment. She opened the cupboard door and found the cat looking at her directly. She was terrorised by this, feeling that the cat was accusing her, and she felt unable to cope with the level of accusation, as though it went through her. Her acute pain and mortification returned and she shut the door, leaving the cat still incarcerated.

In her adolescence, repeated experiences of sensitivity to pain led to the same configuration of attempting to shut out the identified source of the pain, and then feeling overwhelmed by facing the resulting hostility and rage now located in the other. In feeling hurt or wounded by any painful experience, however slight, tremendous hatred, which threatened to take her apart from the inside, was stirred up. She withdrew into a solitary, lonely state, in which daydreams of overcoming human pain, such as achieving immortal recognition as a great person, occupied her mind, or, alternatively she took drugs and alcohol, primarily to remove herself from this intolerable predicament. Return to the world of others was then feared, as others were invested with feeling intense hatred towards her.

In her therapy, the predicament was repeated in patterns where either she or I felt shut in and trapped. On occasions she missed her sessions without informing me, and I found myself feeling intensely troubled, and, at times suffocating, rather like the cat shut in the cupboard, waiting for release either by her arrival or by the end of the session. When Judith occupied the position of the cat, she experienced panic attacks, which had an intensely claustrophobic quality, so that, for example, she suddenly felt the need to get out of where ever she was, and unable to control her mind, her thoughts and feelings. Judith was aware that she was being attacked from within, and that she had no one, in her mind, to reach out to. Her 'objects' had become suffused with hatred. In recounting these experiences, Judith was desperate, feeling fearful that one day she would have a panic attack from which she would not re-emerge, as if being shut in a cupboard forever. On other occasions she felt that if she faced herself, she would descend into a bottomless, awful and intolerable depression, a pain which would be beyond endurance.

Judith was facing a sense of breakdown. Her sensitivity to pain, her narcissistic sensibilities and the feeling of being overwhelmed by her emotional experiences were accompanied, in a rather hidden way, by severe judgements on the self and others. These led to a cycle of retaliatory manoeuvres; the cat should suffer for hurting her; she hurt because the cat suffered; the cat did not wish to repair, or forgive; she experienced new hatred, and retaliated again, and so on. Sense is made of these interactions if they are thought of as projective identification, in which

Judith and the cat had a similar identity, which was reversible. The violence of her splitting led to a nightmare-like internal and external world from which the only escape was some kind of annihilation of the mind or the body. At the same time, the overwhelming fear was of annihilation, being trapped forever in a psychotic part of her mind, an eternal panic attack. She felt she was at risk of being trapped inside her object, and she continually tried to pull away, but then she found that this merely brought about a repetition of panic, or, alternatively, depression. Depression, which she felt to be intolerable and unbearable, was prominent when she was more in contact with others, and vulnerable, or when she herself questioned her own grandiose daydreams.

The image of the cat concretised and made solid an emotional predicament. The absence of containment of emotions, and problems of self–other differentiation, led to a confused and intolerable state. It was possible to see confusion of inner and outer and the cycles of projective identification. There was the absence of an outside perspective, of someone (a 'third' person) who would disentangle internal and external, reaffirm boundaries and the difference between inside and outside, and make an attempt to transform the emotionality – especially in Judith's panicky state, in which, almost, a pure culture of hatred existed. In this sense, the concreteness of the cat imagery stood for a failure in the container–contained relationship, in which instead of reverie there was the refusal of both ingress and invasiveness. Emotions in a world without a container are homeless and potentially attacking, or invading.

Bion described 'beta elements' as 'things' which travel, like missiles, through space, looking for somewhere to land. These are not thoughts but parts of the personality, which have been disowned with the aim of not facing painful reality, or transforming or modifying frustration:

> Beta elements are not amenable to use in dream thoughts but are suited for use in projective identification. They are influential in producing acting out. They are objects that can be evacuated or used for a kind of thinking that depends in manipulation of what are felt to be things in themselves as if to substitute such manipulations for words or ideas. (Bion 1962 p. 6)

Projective identification, used in this sense, is not so much about communicating, more about stripping the personality of everything with which it feels encumbered, so that frustration, disappointment and disillusion do not have to be faced. These projective identifications *may* be used as communication, by therapists who are prepared to be permeated by these feelings, in order to try and think. The length of time it takes to return the projections in modified form, so that the patient may begin to think for her/himself, means that the risk of enactment is high, and the acceptance of the return of the projections depends also on the development in the therapeutic relationship of a sense of the dependability and reliability of the therapist, which the patient can respond to without this being too threatening. In other words, there needs to be a non-psychotic part of the personality which can be working with the therapist.

Working with psychotic adolescents

Dubinsky (1999) has discussed three adolescents who broke down and 'crossed the frontier into psychotic and borderline states' (p. 170). Each of these is discussed within a familial context, so that Dubinsky concludes that they shared features in common – 'the mother was emotionally unavailable, the father was distant, rejecting or cruel' – and she carefully follows the chain of events which led to the breakdown. Thus Debbie, 18, became ill under the pressure of school examinations, when her fragility as a child who seemed not to have parental protection and her projection of her own rage and jealousy into others created a world in which

> painful and frightening similarities between her two worlds became increasingly blatant. In her phantasy world she was absorbed in violent, exciting phantasies in which she was the victim. In real life she became an easy target for playground bullies and later for her abusive boyfriends. (p. 153)

All three adolescents had 'an incapacity to withstand psychic pain in the absence of a containing maternal object' (p. 170). Thomas, 17, suffered from panic attacks. His father had left the family when he was 10 and his grandmother also died at this time. 'Death, ugliness and a tremendous sense of unfairness and loss seemed to have suddenly invaded Thomas' world', so that he felt growth and life was impossible. He found sexuality frightening, so that when he started to have a girlfriend he wanted this more from the point of view of finding another way of merging with mother than as an adult sexual relationship. He was terrified of sex, so that the prospect of having sex with his girlfriend triggered a revival of his panic, and thus he felt he was falling apart.

Dubinsky emphasises that Thomas' problems revolved around his repudiation of masculinity and his wish not to be a man. He had 'identified with a pathetic and fragile male figure' so that all his aggression, rage and violence were projected into 'macho' males, whom he tried to see as 'other'. This account comes close to the view of adolescent breakdown held by the Laufers' (1984), in that Thomas's difficulty in identifying with his father led to him to renounce masculinity. However, Dubinsky's account also emphasises the intolerance of frustration and disappointment, and the process whereby the internal world of the adolescent is subject to violent fragmentation. The experience she records of her experience of working with these patients is important. In working with the third adolescent, Tania, 19, she

> felt violently controlled by her and at times almost immobilised. The atmosphere could feel threatening. For a long time, I felt I could hardly speak of our relationship, of her need for help, of feelings of helplessness. I felt she would want to hate me, get up, leave and never return. All these feelings needed to be lodged in me. I felt impotent, inadequate, small, excluded. It was only when Tania was more trusting of me and felt that I wouldn't abandon her that I could start talking to her about these feelings and we could think together about the underlying fear that her envy, competitiveness and possessiveness would destroy us both.

Thus the 'missile'-like projections from Tania at first need to find a home in the therapist, though these cannot be spoken about for some time, and the therapist experiences the intense pressure of being used in a very concrete, bodily way as a recipient of projections. Premature returning of projections would be experienced as extremely invasive and attacking – like being looked at by an angry cat, to refer back to Judith.

Fragmentation of the self

Breakdown in adolescence begins with the failure of the 'contact barrier' to differentiate inside and outside, internal and external, past and present, conscious and unconscious. In relation to the social world, the individual projects outwards, either in a more benign, communicative way or through the launching of missiles, in the form of split off parts of the self. Two particular situations where intense primitive forms of projective identification produce madness are war and racism. This statement is true in reverse; racism and war produce primitive forms of projective identification. Racism constitutes a distinctive kind of madness in which reality and true sameness – being human – are denied while instead the 'empty category' (Rustin 1991) of race becomes a receptacle (rather than a container – there is no alpha function) for split-off envy and hatred. Social groups 'contain' psychotic aspects and anxieties. In some times, which may be thought of as well functioning, these aspects are kept under control or institutionalised. However, some madness is evident even in these times. According to Segal (1995), 'groups behave in a way which in an individual would be considered mad; for instance, almost invariably groups are self-idealising, grandiose and paranoid' (p. 194). In particular, this is seen in 'national' groups. In times of turbulence, and the conditions of late modernity, the stability of groups is always in question, so that there is a high propensity for mutual 'invasion'. That is, the group infiltrates the individual and vice versa. In contexts of racism and war, the group impacts on the individual by breaking through the contact barrier, and this is apparent through the presence of a 'virtual' war in the home, through TV. During the Gulf War I observed a family where the TV, playing constantly, showed missiles being launched and landing, causing destruction. In the family, feeding of the one-year-old baby resembled a war zone as mother, attempting to gain control of the baby's mouth, insisted that the food-refusing baby ate. Spoonfuls of food became missiles which were treated to the interception of the baby's anti-missile devices – a tensely closed mouth and spitting. The father, returning home after the meal, commented that it looked like a bomb had gone off. Bick (1968, 1986) wrote about the need for a 'psychic skin' to keep together the fragmenting parts of the infant's mind. At the boundary between the inside/family life and the outside/political group there is no functioning contact barrier, and the inside is not held in a skin. Alternatively, a fragile skin is burst through the invasion of the social world, or a thick skin is impervious and therefore unable to respond to the external situation of danger (or opportunity).

Suicidal subjects

In adolescence there is a close connection between psychotic anxieties and suicidality. That is not to say that suicidal adolescents are psychotic, but that the experience of breakdown may be experienced as leading to cessation of development, through the death of the mind (psychosis) or the body (suicide). The combination of the two are vividly illustrated in Anderson's (1999) example of a young man, who made many serious suicide attempts and said that he

> imagined jumping out of a window and flying away leaving his battered and scarred body to fall to the ground. This was not an ordinary religious belief, but a delusion that he could solve his terrible internal state by creating a split between two parts of himself. (p. 165)

The delusion of outliving the body, which Campbell and Hale (1991) call the 'surviving self', indicates the difference between psychosis and suicide as an outcome for adolescent breakdown, in which suicide aims to 'solve' the psychic problem through destruction of the body. Splitting the body and the mind – an idea incidentally 'embodied' in western thought as Cartesian dualism – is the key to suicide, and the relationship with the body is central to understanding suicide. Adolescents at risk of psychosis are often suicidal, but suicide is not the outcome in many cases. Suicidal adolescents are not always manifestly 'psychotic', but there is an element of suicidal thinking in which there is an avoidance of reality, and this can become delusional.

Working with suicide risk

Working with adolescents who are suicidal means being exposed to intense and extreme emotions. These include predominantly anxiety, guilt, a sense of responsibility and fear, both for the adolescent and for oneself. Suicide risk is an important and complex aspect of working with adolescents; it is a high-profile social issue following the international concern about rising rates of suicide, particularly among young men. Suicidality is highly problematic to work with for it is highly unpredictable – literally, prediction of suicide is an inexact science – and because it appears to be essentially heterogeneous. In other words there are multiple or plural 'kinds' of suicidality rather than it being associated with one clinical feature. In psychiatric terms suicide transcends diagnostic categories, and in psycho-social terms there are a number of different 'categories' of suicidal adolescents. As Freud noted, commenting on the complexity of suicide, referring to one of his cases, a young woman of 18 who had made a serious suicide bid, 'several quite different motives, all of great strength, must have co-operated to make such a deed possible' (Freud 1920 p. 163).

Case example: Sonia

Sonia, 17, referred herself for therapy on the advice of her doctor, and wrote a letter in which she said that she took an overdose because 'she gave up on life'. Her passive hopelessness was immediately striking. She was a very distinctive young woman. She had never known her father, of Chinese origins, and during her adolescence, coinciding with her mother becoming very preoccupied with a relationship and more unavailable for Sonia, she had developed an increasing curiosity about him. This curiosity developed in a context of thinking that nothing she could find out would be good. She developed a number of thoughts about her father, that he was dead, a drug addict, a member of a Triad group. She felt increasingly that he had abandoned her, and that she was worthless. She then herself abandoned her efforts to find him, and, at this point, she took an overdose and 'gave up on life'. Feeling hopeless about herself, she was attacked from within by a cruel, raging, damaged, and sadistic father who seemed to tell her she was useless and worthless.

In this case, the problem of suicidality was out in the open. An attempt had been made and the task was to understand the complex processes involved in this young woman's predicament. This situation can be contrasted with those where a suicide bid occurs without previous history, near the beginning of therapeutic contact. The predictability of *knowing* that the adolescent is suicidal is replaced by suicidality exploding into the work with sudden and shocking rapidity.

Case example: Gemma

Gemma was a bright, vivacious and attractive girl of 18 when she was referred for psychotherapy by a school counsellor. There was no indication of suicidal risks in this referral. Gemma's early adolescence was characterised by risk-taking behaviour and early sexual experiences. She idealised her parents and felt guilty about her behaviour, feeling that she constantly let them down. She seemed quite cut off from her own feelings and quite split between a sense of herself as being very successful, especially in her schoolwork, and one of being a burden and a failure. She seemed to try to manage these feelings by playing down their importance to her. She was very sceptical about her therapy, minimised her problems and tried to maintain a superficial attachment to her therapist. She missed sessions, and she was barely engaged in her therapy.

After five sessions, spanning eight weeks (including the missed sessions), she said – not immediately, but some minutes into the session – that she had overdosed since the last session the previous week. She said she had been at a party, and her current boyfriend had ignored her. Feeling he was involved with someone else, she went home and took between 30 and 40 paracetamol tablets. Her parents heard her vomiting and she was taken to hospital. She said that she had told the hospital that she was in therapy and she was discharged.

The sense of detachment was quite stunning. It is not much of an exaggeration to say she finished her story and went on to the next subject. I thought, rather irrationally perhaps, that had I not been able to be at her session that day I might never have heard about this. This thought mirrored the fragility with which her overdosing was found by her parents after a serious suicide bid.

Gemma refused to discuss the reasons for the overdose in more detail on the grounds that she had not, and did not, have any suicidal ideas at all. She did not know why she took the paracetamol, and she never formulated to herself the idea that she *felt* suicidal. She did have to admit that her actions showed she *was*, or had been, suicidal. She was however concerned that she had set a very bad example for her younger sisters, and she felt guilty about hurting her parents, who had been good to her. The feelings of revenge and murderousness towards others, which had surfaced in her suicide bid, became almost instantly inaccessible.

The impact of Gemma's reporting her suicide bid was intensely alarming, and set in train two almost parallel but equally urgent trains of thought. The first, stemming from a sense of responsibility and guilt, both realistic and omnipotent, of a failure to know, protect and control the suicidality, was to analyse whether some clue to the suicidality had been overlooked. The second was to attempt to think about the meaning and causes of this bid.

The sense of responsibility is partly a professional response to a serious situation. Should there have been some greater awareness of the potential for suicidality and should more action have been taken? Partly, it is driven by a wish to escape blame. This is heightened in organisations, which, operating under the impact of the 'logic of control and inspection', as discussed in Chapter 5, become omnipotent when fear of outcomes becomes the sole driver within them.

The stressfulness of working with suicidal adolescents, and being engaged in the assessment of suicidality, cannot be overstated. It does demand a particular kind of containment for staff, in which the purposeful discussion of cases, the capacity to make judgements of risk and the capacity to maintain a perspective are paramount. The sense of perspective is gained, in part, by making a difficult and delicate separation of responsibilities. The therapist's responsibilities are not total, and the adolescent has some responsibilities too, but the delicacy lies in maintaining a sense of therapeutic boundaries in a field of knowledge – suicide risk – which is unpredictable, complex and uncertain.

Suicidal dynamics in adolescents: cruelty

We can compare the two cases above – Gemma and Sonia – to consider some of the key suicidal dynamics in adolescence.

Sonia's situation is striking for the immediate presentation of a passive hopelessness, a quiet, resigned despair. Interacting with this is a vicious, cruel and attacking part of her which seems to be identified with her father, and which seems to tell her she is worthless. In *The Ego and the Id* (Freud 1923) Freud discussed an internal conflict as follows:

> the ego gives itself up because it feels itself hated and persecuted by the super-ego, instead of loved. When the ego finds itself in an excessive real danger which it believes itself unable to overcome by its own strength, it is bound to draw the same conclusion. It sees itself deserted by all protecting forces and lets itself die. (Freud 1923 p. 58)

In this pitiful state, the ego cannot raise a single cry against the accusations, and has to succumb. It is a powerful description of a precondition for suicide; that for a moment, or longer, there can be no voice to be heard from within on the side of life.[1] Hopelessness and despair are implicit in this state of helplessness. The sadistic attacks of the super-ego and the helplessness of the ego are complementary aspects, suggesting that while either sadistic attacks on the self or hopelessness may form the presentation of the suicidal state, each presumes the existence of the other. A helpless, giving-up ego indicates the presence of a savage, merciless super ego and vice versa.

The merciless cruelty of the superego may be related in Sonia's case to the experience she had in her mind about being abandoned by her father, as a very cruel act on his part. In this way she had identified internally with the abandoning father. This follows Freud's original and enduring ideas about the problem of mourning (Freud 1917). When a loss involves an ambivalently loved and hated other, instead of grief and separation taking place, the other is taken in and identified with, so that the other is felt to be a part of the self. When the identification is with a cruel and attacking other – or alternatively someone who has been cruelly attacked – the impact is that the self is attacked and hated from within and this gives rise to the self-reproaches of depressive (melancholic) individuals. When the identification is with a remorselessly cruel 'object' the result can be that there appears to be no escape from the relentlessness of these attacks, except through death.

Suicidal dynamics: getting rid of the pain

Gemma's suicidality appears differently from Sonia's. Whereas Sonia is aware of despair, and suicidal wishes, Gemma is not, and her detachment from her suicidal intention creates a strong sense of denial. Gemma shows how sudden, impulsive and explosive, uncontained feelings of rejection, abandonment and revenge can be triggered, and how much this suicidal behaviour was linked with Gemma not being able to know about these feelings and her *inner* relationships. She was aware of sudden, intensive feelings of rejection and abandonment, which she seemed to feel she needed to get rid of immediately. This represents a violent defence against perceptions of vulnerability and need in herself, and is turned against herself through her body. The brief, fleeting contact with a sense of vulnerability and need threatened to humiliate and overthrow a sense of a competent, independent and omnipotent self.

This explosive kind of suicidality, in which depression is not easily visible, is often the kind encountered in young suicidal males. The absence of visible or acknowledged depression in suicidal adolescents is puzzling, until the difference between depressive illness and depressive pain is held in mind. Depressive illness occurs, according to Klein, through an inability to manage the pains of the depressive position. Thus there is a difference between the pain of awareness of damage done, psychically, to the object, and the anxiety and pain that arises from feeling persecuted. Bell (2000) points out a different kind of depression, 'a particular kind of tormenting psychic pain which arises from the feeling of being internally persecuted by the recriminations of damaged objects – as if, so to speak, they are saying 'we are all suffering, look what you have done to us' (p. 25, n. 1).

Case example: Gary

Gary, 16, felt furious about feeling excluded by his parents from their separate lives, in which each of them had younger children. He robbed, menacingly a group of smaller boys. He said he was not at all remorseful about this. However, during the following few days he got into violent arguments with his mother and a teacher, which culminated, on his father's birthday, in his mother telling him to leave home. He then made a suicide bid.

Gary made active the experience of which he was first a passive recipient, that is of feeling 'robbed' of the love of his parents, and replaced by new siblings. He then intensified his sense of being excluded by arguing with mother and getting himself rejected, again. He then turned this round again, to 'rob' his parents of their child, himself. The torturing kind of depression is somewhere in this configuration, and both powerfully acted on and reacted against.

The lack of space, or time, between the experience of rejection and the suicide attempt in Gemma's case indicates an impulsive inability to wait, while her evacuation of these intolerable feelings was directed into her body. Thus, as in psychotic anxieties, a missile of projective identification was being launched; however, rather than being directed into the outside world, searching for an external object or just being launched into outer space, it was aimed, first, into herself, through her body; then, by thus taking herself hostage, she indirectly targeted someone else, who would be left to suffer for or repent of the lack of love and consideration she, Gemma, had been given. The impulsivity thus reveals a particular relationship between the container and the contained, in which the container is put under terrific pressure to respond to an impossible request, immediately and fully. This is a configuration of internal terrorism, which can be particularly powerful and chilling when it is put ruthlessly into practice.

Many adolescents have suicidal ideas, from time to time, but far fewer are seriously worried about them and fewer still act on them. In contrast, those who are seriously troubled by suicidality, and likely to act, are in serious inner and interpersonal difficulties. Adolescent suicidality constitutes a crisis of inner relationships, and adolescents who are at risk of suicide are not passing through a transient phase of difficulty which is cured by time (Perret-Catipovic and Ladame 1998).

Suicidal internal dynamics have been thought of as a series of distinct but overlapping internal relationships. The 'motive force' in suicide is found in the following relationships (Campbell and Hale 1991).

Merger The aim of the suicide bid is to solve a problem of separation, in which being separate is intolerable and being in intimate contact is engulfing. The 'solution' is to idealise a state of merger, or fusion. For example:

> Penny, 16, described a difficult relationship with her mother, who was critical and attacking, calling her 'bad' and 'dirty', and at times humiliated her in public. In her misery, Penny fantasised about being united with a star, which she called 'her star'. She thought how she might be transported to be with the star, and contemplated a suicide bid by jumping from a bridge.

Revenge As discussed above in the case of Gary, revenge, on the principle of the talion law, is the 'solution' for the pains of being left or abandoned. There is an aim of triumphing through others' remorse, and of making parents, in particular, regret not having loved the son or daughter better.

Self-punishment The aim is to resolve conflict in relationships through punishing the self. Freud (1924) wrote of self-punishment that, 'in order to provoke punishment from [the super-ego], the masochist must do what is inexpedient, must act against his own interests, must ruin the prospects which open out to him in the real world and must, perhaps, destroy his own existence' (p. 169). Often, sexual guilt is involved (Penny, above, was self-punishing as well as merging) and Flaubert's Emma Bovary is an example from literature. Either the self-punishing suicidal individual reaches the point of despair and gives up, or there is a self-sacrificing or atoning quality present.

Elimination The case of Gemma has been discussed as an example of 'elimination' in which the aim is to 'get rid of' the painful state of turbulence. The delusion is that this preserves the individual through expulsion of the unwanted states of mind.[2]

Dicing with death Adolescents are particularly likely to be found 'dicing with death'. On one level, it means experimenting with risks and taking an omnipotent view of things. In suicidal situations, the adolescent aims to overcome despair, misery, or failure through undertaking a risky enterprise which might end catastrophically, but which may also produce a high. At the extreme the stakes are highest, and then the 'game' is like Russian roulette, when death is not feared. Parental care is rejected and replaced by an omnipotent gamble. The suicidal dicing-with-death adolescent oscillates between misery and abjection on one side and manic invulnerability on the other. The drug-user's 'unreliable container' is close to this configuration, and drugs are often used as the means of the 'gamble'.

Case example: Nick

Nick, 17, told me that he had crashed his friend's motorbike. He was not hurt, but he seemed to be communicating to me that he had felt the need to do something which was quite dangerous. I raised with him the fact that he had previously told me that he sometimes had suicidal thoughts. He said he did not have an active wish to kill himself, but when he felt particularly bad he would take on a gamble in which he might get damaged, or killed, but which might also lead to a sense of triumph.

Suicidal relationship to the body

These internal configurations are thought to power suicidality, though what distinguishes suicidal and self-harming adolescents from others is the relationship they have with the body. Earlier, in Chapter 2, I have discussed the adolescent body as a site for the interplay of internal and socio-cultural experiences of subjectivity, and as a means of resistance. Suicidal adolescent bodies are disowned, hated and felt to be impediments to arriving at more peaceful and less turbulent states of mind (Laufer 1985, Laufer and Laufer 1984, Anderson 1999, Fonagy and Target 1999). Laufer and Laufer (1984) emphasise that suicidal adolescents dislike or hate the body. They discuss the way the development of the body in adolescence brings about unwanted separation from childhood, and thus how the development of sexuality is hated as confirming the loss of childhood and the emergence into the adult world.

A suicide attempt causes a rupture, which attacks meaning and freezes subjectivity (Ladame 2001). Painful phantasies and emotional experiences are denied and annihilated by the bid. Thus there is a loss of alpha function, and the skin–containment is also attacked, ruptured or obliterated. The suicidal adolescent is more likely to be defended in relation to the body, not knowing about its qualities, not thinking or feeling the rhythms and perceptions that are located in it. Suicidal adolescents are more likely to objectify the body, and to split it from the mind, creating a Cartesian fallacy. Foucault thought that resistance meant that there was action on bodies to 'transform themselves in order to attain a certain state of happiness, purity, wisdom, perfection or immortality' (Foucault 1988 p. 18). However, what Foucault had in mind was the maximising of pleasure, beauty and power rather than the destruction of self – and, through the dyadic nature of suicide, the inflicting of terrible pain on others.

Protection from psychosis and suicide

Kennedy (1998) has written that

> the psychotic subject has a precarious subjective organisation, made up of 'loose' elements that can fall apart and can be experienced then as physical objects. Perhaps one could pay more attention to the details of what holds the elements together, the psychic 'glue' so to speak. (p. 188)

In this discussion, both psychotic and suicidal subjects are subject to fragmentation, and yet the plurality, multiplicity and diversity of modern life create potentially fragmentary experiences which require reflection so that some kind of order can be made from turbulence. In the inner world, especially in the Bion–Bick model, the experience of the mother's reverie pulls together the potentially fragmenting infant, who thus gets to know both the sense-providing and integrating function of the mother and also the fragmentary state which she protects her/him from.

Amiel (2001) describes a young man, John, 19, who after a psychotic breakdown, arrived for his therapy one day carrying a

> tatty carrier bag which split, pouring disconnected bits of his life on to the floor; old letters, combs, rotting food, medication. Together we taped up the bag and slowly put all the bits back into it. Much later in his therapy he was able to see this moment as a metaphor for the process which he had undertaken and the reintegration he had been able to begin to achieve. (p. 31)

Kennedy suggests that attention should be paid to the psychic 'glue'; Amiel's example is a vivid instance of the concreteness of the psychotic breakdown, and the jumble of objects which are unlinked, meaninglessly, in the carrier bag, a container, which itself is split and likely to leak its contents. The suicidal subject aims to break the container and to fragment the contents. Amiel also shows, as did Dubinsky, whose work was discussed earlier in this chapter, the demand on the therapist to hold these events in mind over time, before a more symbolic form of communication can be achieved or regained.

Containment is a binding, linking force and process, which problematises fragmentation and aims to provide connections between parts through meaning and symbolisation. The 'skin' is a boundary which has to bear the pressure and stresses of holding onto fragments. Linking with another offers a potential for hope, and self-containment:

> An 18-year-old, subject to self-destructive attacks on herself, became explosively furious and impulsively decided to throw herself in front of a passing car. At the pavement's edge she stopped and thought to herself that she did not wish to jeopardise her therapy.

On the brink of potential self-destruction, she found a different voice in her mind, which pulled her back, into a connectedness with her therapist, with the idea that it mattered. Being felt to be kept in mind, she could protect herself (precariously) through keeping in her mind an integrating and meaningful relationship.

Summary

- Psychotic breakdown in adolescence is discussed in terms of the processes in which the domains of inside and outside, conscious and unconscious are confused and broken down, through the operation of violent projective identification.
- Psychotic experiences are heightened in post-modernity, so that a fragmented and dangerous external world may be internalised, as well as a fragmented inner world projected into the external world. 'Psychotic anxieties' are widely expe-

rienced, but these do not lead to psychosis unless there is a failure of containment.

- The absence of containment of dangerous aspects of the self leads to a confused and intolerable, concretely experienced inner world. Bion's concept of beta elements is discussed to make sense of the concreteness of these states of mind.
- The therapist working with potentially psychotic adolescents will need to be able to take in the unbearable states of mind which are projected, and to hold on to them for some time. Case examples were given to illustrate these processes.
- Suicidal adolescents split the body and the mind, and can develop delusional ideas that killing the body solves the emotional problems that underlie suicidality.
- Suicidal adolescents present heterogeneously. Some are depressed and know consciously that they are desperate. Others may be more cut off from their emotionality and seem to deny their own suicidality. Case examples were used to illustrate these differences, and discussed in terms of the dynamics of cruelty and getting rid of the pain.
- Psychotic and suicidal adolescents are subject to fragmentation internally, and containment helps to bring these fragmented parts together, providing connections between parts of the self, or psychic glue, which acts as a protection from suicide and psychosis.

LEAVING HOME

This chapter explores the way adolescents enter adulthood. The piecemeal transitions in contexts of contemporary society mean that adolescents take different routes into adulthood, and face diverse risks and opportunities. The impact on identity of taking up more adult roles is discussed.

Do adolescents still leave home?

Adolescents now leave home in stages. Unlike the simple transition from family of origin to family of destination, the transitions from school to employment, and away from the family home, are subject to a fragmentary process. More often than not, there are repeated leavings and returns, with intermediary stopping-off places and arrangements. There are, therefore, comparable piecemeal internal processes of entering adulthood. Diversity externally and internally is the hallmark of ways in which adolescents become 'more adult', and this is probably a more meaningful way to describe the late-adolescent transitional process than the traditional formulation of leaving home.

Adolescents are dependent upon, and subject to, economic possibilities and restrictions, for education, housing and employment. Rapid changes in all these spheres have destabilised the context of the process to adulthood, producing 'difference, exclusion and marginalisation' (Giddens 1991 p. 6). Adolescents 'embark on journeys into adulthood which involve a wide variety of routes, many of which appear to have uncertain outcomes' (Furlong and Cartmel 1997 p. 7). Thus the experience of leaving home is experienced as a 'calculative attitude to the open possibilities of action, positive and negative, with which, as individuals and globally, we are confronted in a continuous way with contemporary social existence' (Giddens 1991 p. 28). Leaving home becomes individualised as traditional structures and institutions are obscure; everything is presented as a possibility and yet constraints loom from all sides. Loss, as well as risks and hazards, looms large.

Facing loss and separation

Loss in the process of transition from adolescence to adulthood is experienced in relation to the social world. Becoming engaged in the opportunities, constraints and risks of adulthood ushers in an intensification of the awareness of the loss of the past, of the ending of childhood. Waddell (1998) emphasises the enormity of the late adolescent task:

> It is a time of hope and expectation, but for many, also of extreme sadness and distress, and even of breakdown for the few who find themselves unequal to the task . . . At the heart of the matter lies the degree of the person's capacity to experience loss, a loss especially stark as childhood is definitively left behind and engagement with the adult world becomes a necessity. (pp. 158–9)

It is the urgency impelled by the non-negotiable fact of transition to adulthood, to take up adult roles and positions, that propels so many late adolescents to therapy. Whereas in early adolescence engagement in therapy and other kinds of responsibilities, are avoidable unless parents or school are very definite about their necessity, late adolescents often refer themselves for therapy. Many of the examples of young people in therapy discussed in this book fall into this category. Though the transition is now often deferred – the examples of Maria and Howard in Chapter 1 are cases in point – it cannot be put off for ever. Erikson seemed very aware of the urgency and the enormity of the transition when he wrote about the way the individual developed

> a new kind of identification, achieved in absorbing sociability and in competitive apprenticeship among his age mates. These new identifica-

tions are no longer characterised by the playfulness of childhood and the experimental zest of youth; with dire urgency they force the young individual into choices and decisions which will with increasing immediacy lead to commitments for life. The task to be performed here by the young person and his society is formidable. (Erikson 1968 p. 155)

In contemporary contexts the 'commitments for life' appear to be those of engaging in the calculation of risks and opportunities in a range of individualised decisions. The transition into adulthood takes many forms, and there are many different kinds of late adolescent transition – depending on the contexts. There are even risks and hazards in deferring work and responsibilities, through the institutionalised moratorium of the gap year.

Case example: Peter

Peter was contemplating a period of travel during his gap year. He felt propelled to get away from home. Tentatively he tried to discuss his plans with me, but inevitably he stumbled on the same problem, that he both wished to get away from his therapy, and thus to evade his difficulties, and was frightened of leaving. However, his plans progressed and he announced boldly that he had made the decision to travel. Then he crumpled before his fears about leaving. He said he was ready, and not ready. He said his friends had been winding him up by saying that he would be back within a week. He asked what I would decide about his therapy. I said that we both had something to contribute to that decision. I added that if I said I'd see him when he got back I would not be taking into account his anxieties, expressed through his friends, that he might need me before then. If I said I'd see him next week as usual I would be undermining his attempts to make his plans succeed. He said he would phone if he came back early.

Peter's plans were for a temporary absence, rather than a permanent departure, but they were nevertheless full of anxiety, and combined constructive and destructive aspects. He was anxious about himself and also about how he would be thought about in his absence. Would I keep a space for him, or would I fill it with someone else? This appeared rather delicate. Too fulsome an offer from me could lead him to feel trapped and subject to my wishes; not enough of an offer would leave him feeling unsure whether he had a place in therapy, and in my mind. Peter was involved in a calculative process, engaging with subjective risks and weighing up the options.

The anxieties involved in the late adolescent transition demonstrate the falsity of the traditional view of adolescence. This has been satirised as being 'kick started by puberty and cruis[ing] slowly to a halt at adult identity, the point at which the petrol is getting low and we need to think about saving it for the long, straight road ahead' (Van Heeswyk 1997 p. 3).

Positioning as adults

The positioning of adolescents as adults occurs within the power/knowledge discourse. In the context of wide, sweeping changes in the social structures affecting transitions into adulthood, adolescents 'are increasingly held accountable for their own fates' (Furlong and Cartmel 1997 p. 8) and yet there are strong external and internal forces which the adolescent is 'subject to'. There is often an illusion of choice and control, and a gap between possibility and expectation. Knowledge, as educational knowledge and credentials, is a powerful factor in the transition into adulthood.

We have seen how Mrs J's students (Chapter 5) were abject at the imminent prospect of leaving school with no qualifications, and therefore feeling quite vulnerable in taking up adult roles. This were extremely realistic of them, since one effect of radical changes in the social context of late adolescence is to place educational attainment at the centre of the complex routes into adulthood.

Exams are a rites of passage into adulthood, increasing the tension and anxiety about performance, and highlighting the difference between those equipped to succeed and those who are more vulnerable. George (Chapter 6) did not take GCSEs, because of his state of mind at the time, when he was preoccupied with the difficulties in his family. With the underlying agenda of providing a passage into adulthood, exams test the authenticity of the adolescent's credentials for making it in the adult world. Success in doing and passing exams provides reassurance that the appearance fits the reality, that the adolescent has 'qualified' for adult status. Success positions the adolescent as more adult, which is a more powerful state, and yet brings with it new vulnerability and fragility, as s/he faces future uncertain-

ties. Anxiety about exams can rock the sense of self, testing internalisations and containment. This can become acute if it seems to
point out to the adolescent that something is wrong, that the test,
symbolically, is only the first of many in adult life. Samantha
(Chapter 7), for example, lost a sense of herself as a competent,
successful student during the year of her A levels. Her fear of loss
of control began to become manifest when she got behind with
her work and then she felt panic that she could never catch up.
This is not to say that the exams were a cause of her breaking
down, for that would be superficial. The tension and pressure
around exams, together with the underlying meaning that they
led to separation through leaving home and going to university,
revealed problems and weaknesses in her identity.

Taking a driving test comes a close second to exams, in terms
of a ritualistic passage to adulthood. Adolescents are often
extremely crushed by failure and thrilled by success. Failure
seems to stand for a judgement, for a refusal to be allowed to
enter adulthood, and enjoy the fruits of adult power – driving –
and the driving examiner can be represented as a demonic figure,
guarding the gates to paradise. Driving, that is, travelling as
nature intended, as Meg Ryan put it in the film *French Kiss*, may
be more important to some young people than having a home
(Joseph Rowntree Foundation 2001). In this case, leaving home
becomes a less significant goal than owning a car. Both however lead to the possession of keys, which symbolically confer
power. The power/knowledge concept points to the relationship
between self-knowledge and power. To have an awareness of
oneself, one's subjectivity is the means to power/knowledge, but
trying to respond to one's sense of vulnerability by seeking more
powerful positions can lead to repetitive behaviour. Driving tests
can be repeatedly failed by adolescents who 'know' that they can
drive, but whose performative skills let them down. Omnipotence breaks down under the experience of pressure from external realities. Anxieties about taking up a more adult position,
fragmentation in the face of these anxieties and underlying
Oedipal competitiveness provide deeper explanations.

In the context of the late adolescent transition, there is a
movement towards becoming, which is harnessed to adolescent
ideas of knowing that certain positions are desirable. Taking up
more powerful subject positions means losing, or giving up on,

other positions which are less powerful, but allow access to being dependent. Relinquishment of these relationships means experiencing loss. Thus vulnerability may be heightened (see Urwin 1998 ch. 2). Relationships between adolescents and adults, including therapists, are important in developing what Noam calls 'contexts of affirmation', sorting out realities from omnipotent illusions and providing a space to think about the meaning and implications of proposed routes. In the late adolescent transition, the process of becoming a subject is one of completing, testing, and monitoring how the impact of adult positioning will affect identity. At this point the adolescent is acutely aware of a gap between her/himself, and others. This leads to anxiety, and an increase in the need for containment. The openness of this moment, the imperative for action and the opportunity to reflect both back in time and on one's future prospects brings to bear a sense of what Erikson thought of as the enormity of the project of adolescence.

Becoming positioned as adults replaces leaving home. In the movement from leaving adolescence to entering adulthood, four aspects of 'becoming' are important:

• becoming a student
• becoming a sexual partner
• becoming a parent
• becoming a worker

These four aspects are subject to wide diversities in terms of the meaning of the experience – working, partnership, parenting and student role. Diverse routes into each of them ensure that the meanings of these experiences need to be located firmly in the individual and social context.

Becoming a student

Becoming a student used to be a traditional way for middle-class adolescents to partly leave home and enter into a last stage of childhood. Contemporary adolescence is different, and the role of student is taken up by a majority of young people, in diverse ways. The explosion of the student population is one of the significant changes in the landscape for young people, alongside the centrality of education as the primary source of power/knowledge. Becoming a student is a diverse experience, which raises other aspects of the late transition, especially with regard to relationships with family and with boy/girlfriends, and also with regard to choices and decisions about future directions. Thus becoming a student is always part of a field of transition. Many of the case examples in this book discuss the processes of separating that are linked with student roles. Howard, in Chapter 1, experienced a sense of fragmentation at the end of his university experience, and the uncertainties of identity began to impact upon him then, rather than earlier in adolescence. Some young people experience the end of a university course as returning them, painfully, to an uncertain and difficult set of experiences, in which they are often vulnerable, facing turbulent and rebuffing contact with the adult world of work, and limitations to independence from parents. Others may experience the student role as a period of temporary outsidership, which enhances the capacity to reflect and bear emotions and thoughts. The overall effect of the new way that the student role impacts is to lengthen the period of adolescence and to leave young adults facing adolescent issues.

Often, relationships with peers as well as experiences of study are vital aspects of being a student. Some find shared living with other students a supportive and enhancing experience, others that it presents many conflicts within complex group dynamics. Positioning as a student, and in relation to being a student, is central to late adolescence. The way late adolescents engage with the role of student is defining for them, for it is hardly possible to move from adolescence to adulthood without having negotiated a student role of some kind. How the role of student connects with other more adult positions can be seen in the following example, in which becoming a student has a significant effect on the issue of becoming a sexual partner.

Becoming a sexual partner

Case example: Sasha

Sasha's dilemmas about starting university formed an important aspect of her therapy. It meant also working out a relationship with a boyfriend, which was already of long standing but caused her considerable ambivalence. Initially, when she began therapy she felt that she would have to separate from him, recognising at some level within herself that she had become involved in order to avoid the pains of adolescence, rather than making a positive decision to become involved in a sexual partnership.

As her fear of separations began to be held in her therapy, she felt more able to think about a future which might include her boyfriend, and the renegotiations of their relationship which would need to take place. Between them, they did negotiate a way in which they could continue their relationship and both go to different universities, to keep in touch, have time together and also have some elements of separate lives. The precariousness of the separateness was expressed through awareness at everyday levels. For example, Sasha discovered, to her furious disbelief, that her boyfriend's new mobile phone was on a different network from hers. Reluctantly, another aspect of separateness had to be faced.

The painfulness of leaving home was expressed in the ending of her therapy. Was this to be a temporary parting, or a permanent ending? There emerged a qualitative difference between negotiable and non-negotiable facts. On the one hand, she could leave home, go to university, return home and go to see her boyfriend, while he could visit her – so why could she not return to her therapy? I felt extremely mean and cruel in trying to stick to the agreed boundary that the therapy would end. I wondered why I felt this was necessary; often it is possible to arrange for continuing contact, during vacations and so on. I seemed to have pushed myself into a corner, in which to back down would mean feeling humiliated by Sasha's assertions that she knew best, and that I was making a mistake. However, when Sasha spoke about her brother, a different aspect emerged, in that the meaning of separating also meant being left, as an infant, by a mother who had another child. Through this Sasha lost the sense of a space with mother which was just hers. Thus the meaning of separating to go to university was complicated by the influence of the non-negotiable infantile situation, alongside the purely 'adolescent' issue, that her sole space with mother was lost forever when her younger brother was born. The definite ending of the therapy brought the non-negotiable infantile issue to the foreground, and through this differentiation of different kinds of separation and separateness became available for discussion.

The relationship Sasha developed with her boyfriend may have begun as

> a pairing-off, which . . . despite appearances [has] little to do with a genuine transition from adolescent to adult states of mind . . . Indeed such couplings can constitute precisely the opposite; that is, a defensive bonding in the face of anxiety about what stepping into adulthood might really entail (Waddell 1998 p. 158).

In her therapy, Sasha was able to find, with difficulty, and at times agonisingly, a path between two polarities. One polarity was to be stuck in a retreat from adulthood in a relationship which denied separateness. The other was to jettison her boyfriend in a frantic attempt to undo the relationship, because a key motive for the involvement was to retreat from the pains of separateness. The latter would have also caused both of them pain, and could be construed as masochistic. Developing the capacity to become attached and separate was undertaken within the relationship, which became transformed by this process, though still in some ways precariously so. The complexities of becoming repositioned as being in an adult sexual partnership were complicated through growing into them, so to speak, from within the partnership. But, again, that could be defined as an adult quality, that is, the capacity to keep developing within a relationship. For Sasha, taking up an adult subject position in her relationship enabled her to begin to differentiate between infantile and adult aspects of relating.

Case example: Prasad

Prasad had a very different route towards adulthood. When she began university she put thoughts of leaving home and having a relationship out of her mind. She would have liked to live in student accommodation but it would have created too many problems in her Bangladeshi family. Also, she believed that the right course for her was to adhere to traditional cultural values. She was accepting of the limitations this put on her social life, and especially when she felt herself to be in a marginal position with her friends at university. When Prasad started to go out more to see student friends her parents became anxious and followed her, and she was quite upset that they seemed to mistrust her when she was so 'good'. She was also furious that they did not seem to know about her ideology and beliefs. She began to feel that she had to be more rigorously self-reflective, to really be sure that her ideas were her own, and belonged to her, and she realised that as she continued her studies she might change her views. She began to think it would be possible for her to be in a relationship, and this stirred up a fear of difficult conflicts ahead within herself and with her parents.

Prasad had complicated reasons for taking up her traditional and conformist position, and she was anxious about experiencing change within herself, precipitating conflict within herself and in her family. Ghuman (1999 p. 119) gives an example of an Indian girl facing a similar context. She said:

> my father would not let me go away from home to a university in London. Then I suggested that I could stay with my uncle and travel daily to the university. He agreed . . . Then my parents were concerned that I was getting too old (22 years) and they should arrange a match for me. I said 'definitely not from India'. To which they agreed. Then I said: 'Let me finish my diploma course.' After that I turned down several boys and chose the one I really liked; it was a sort of compromise . . . There was never any question of dating, or going out with boys.

For this girl, the move towards adulthood was accompanied by developing a sense of agency through the capacity to negotiate with parents. Prasad began to be more anxious about her internal and intersubjective positions, anticipating and fearing change, but also not withdrawing from the student role which was the crucible for these thoughts and emergent difficulties.

Becoming a parent

The preparation for taking up a parental roles is a complex one, based on separation and differentiation from one's own parents, and the development of a sense of being different from as well as the same as one's parents. Subjectivation, the process of appropriating ownership of one's body, thoughts and passions, depends on achieving 'a mind which is rooted in and yet also distinct from the sources and models of identification that are visible in one's family, or in the wider school and community setting' (Waddell 1998 p. 158). Becoming different from, but having a sense of being the same as, creates the foundations for belonging and individuality, attachment and separation. From this bedrock, taking up the role of parent follows this ordering, and of course, traditionally, requires the prior establishment of a sexual couple. However, vulnerable adolescents take other routes to parenthood. If becoming prematurely involved in a sexual relationship can constitute a retreat from the anxieties of impending adulthood, and also an attempt to become re-positioned as an adult, becoming pregnant may have the same meanings.

Case example: Tanya

Tanya left home at 16, after an argument with her mother. She moved into a house shared by other young people, an 'intermediary house-hold',[1] became pregnant and decided to keep the baby. She did not wish to maintain a relationship with the baby's father. Soon anxiety about her capacity to care for the baby became very high, and the potential risk to the baby led to social work involvement. Tanya was unsupported by her family, her conflicts with her mother increased and conflict pervaded her relationships with professionals. She accepted an offer of individual therapy, and the therapist was able to establish a rapport with her, despite her very strong sense of persecution. The therapeutic rela-tionship provided an important link for Tanya, through the period when child protection procedures were focused on her. When the baby was born she was devoted to her, and her intolerance of frustration reduced, so that she was less volatile and able to put up with a difficult environ-ment and limited support, externally, from her family. The capacity to make a link with her baby, and with her therapist, provided her with a sense of having some internal resources. Resilience emerged in a way that was quite unexpected.

Teenage pregnancy has formed a contemporary 'moral panic'. Usually it is seen in the same way as premature 'coupling', as a way of avoiding the anxieties of adulthood. Ambrose (2001 p. 84) suggests:

Separation usually involves physically leaving home as well as emo-tionally leaving. This is very difficult for many young people, particu-larly if they are enmeshed with their mother. They may be scared of coping alone. A gradual loosening of bonds may be too difficult and pregnancy may be a way to leave. It may be seen as a way to leave home, separate, be seen as a grown up, independent, different. Alternatively since pregnant teenagers often stay with their mothers it may be a way not to leave home, solving the dilemma for the young person. The boyfriend is unimportant in this case. Pregnancy avoids painful choices about the future.

Ambrose provides a wealth of examples which illustrate the role of pregnancy in conflicts between adolescents and, especially, parents. The attitudes of these teenagers range from knowingly seeking to get pregnant to denial of the possibility, hoping it will not happen to them.

Case example: Mary

Mary, a 17-year-old, asked for therapy through her social worker. She was about to leave care, and she had become perturbed by an increasing sense of loss, of not knowing who her father was, and the rejection she had experienced from her mother. The social worker had thoughtfully, over some time, discussed with her the idea of having therapy. When she made the referral, the social worker felt confident that Mary did wish to have therapy, though she also felt that she was quite fragile and anxious about what would happen in her therapy. Mary did attend her first therapy appointment, but between making the referral and the appointment the social worker learned that Mary had become pregnant. Mary was clear she would keep the baby. She did make emotional contact with the therapist in her consultation, but indicated she would not now wish to continue with having therapy.

Mary seemed to have thought about therapy for herself, but to have made a choice to have a baby instead. There did seem to be a sense in which she felt anxiety about the past, for the baby part of her who felt so rejected and needed attention, but facing therapy was too difficult for her. Mary seemed to feel that being in the role of parent to her baby would be more manageable, emotionally, than being actively involved in experiences of her own infancy, in therapy. Tanya, on the other hand, taking a similar route into adulthood, found therapy supported her taking up a more adult position. The anxiety about Tanya when she was pregnant mobilised both responses to potential risks, and support and attentiveness. These had been absent in her earlier adolescence, which she felt to have been particularly abject. Teenagers who become pregnant are likely to be extremely vulnerable, having probably experienced deprivation, abuse and loss of family through being in care (Garnett 1992).

But Tanya's relationship with her baby opened up a negotiable aspect of her and provided her with some opportunities for becoming more grown up, needed and loved (Musick 1993). In the face of limited familial, internal, educational and economic opportunities, parenthood appeared to become a chosen option (Phoenix 1991), which had the opportunities and possibilities as well as the risks and hazards, of a more-adult position, albeit a somewhat precarious one.

The great divide: leaving home, leaving care

The process of leaving home reveals a great divide, in terms of class. Noam (1999 p. 52) points out that 'even in the past, the adolescent moratorium required some money in the bank as well as some educational capital in the home'. The process of leaving adolescence is now more closely tied to educational capital and the capacity of families to support the young person through the vicissitudes of the late adolescent transition:

> The outcome of policies privatizing the welfare of young people on to their families by extending parental responsibilities is that family support is now a crucial factor in determining young people's life chances, and those without it are at the greatest risk. Yet for a variety of reasons, access to family support may have become more difficult. (Jones 1995 p. 12)

Thus young people may remain dependent on families for an extended period of time, and this 'rests on the dubious proposition that families are able and willing to submit to the authority of their parents during this period' (Furlong and Cartmel 1997 p. 52)

Young people whose families cannot offer this support, or who have difficulties within the family, face a different prospect. It remains anomalous that, despite legislation and the development of services for leaving care, the most vulnerable adolescents are required to be more independent earlier than those who have educational and actual capital available to them.

Julia (Chapter 5) was prepared for independence when she was 16. This meant developing practical skills for living alone, and moving into a semi-independent flat. The anxiety about the risks faced by young people leaving care can nudge staff towards colluding with pseudo-independence, hurrying development. Julia found it very difficult to make contact with others emotionally, and to allow contact, which might become painful so that the veneer of maturity masked a desperate internal need for others. Leaving care means that an emotionally deprived adolescent, who has probably been subject to many changes and disruptions, faces the difficult and challenging task of developing the resources to contend with 'independence'. This splits the adolescent into one part that is still a child and another that has to be adult. The adult, independent position is often the more appealing, since the disappointments and pains of relating to parental figures have left mistrust of others, and a painful residue of damage. Anxieties about holding together a self which has not been contained within continuous relationships can leak through the attempt to maintain a sense of self-control.

Case example: John

John had been in foster care until the placement broke down when he was 16. He returned to her mother's care and revived many of the difficulties which had led to him being accommodated when he was nine. John and his mother therefore resumed a conflictual relationship, which was painful for both of them. John asked for a place of his own and was provided with a bedsit. At this point both were in an agonised state of not being able to bear leaving and being left. A therapeutic consultation was arranged for them both to be seen, but separately. In his consultation John was very tearful, crying a great deal about the pain he felt about his mother rejecting him and the pain of leaving her. Towards the end of the interview he started to talk about how much better he felt it would be to be in his own place, and that his move was about to take place. He wrapped himself in his coat, and seemed to tighten it around him, as if to hold himself together. After he left, the therapist was extremely anxious about a delicate and fragile boy, who had gone, unprotected, into the outside world. This was a powerful and evocative worry, raising the question as to whether he would survive. An infant part of John had been left, along with the tears, with the therapist. When

John next returned to see the therapist, he had moved into his flat, and his talk was about college and friends, and he conveyed a sense of an active life connected to his friends.

John put into his therapist a very powerful feeling of being an abandoned baby. The painful mourning of the lost relationship of a child with his mother appeared to free him to take up a more adult position. John was fortunate in the strength of his peer network, and, as he positioned himself as living independently, he gained the benefits of these relationships, and he was able to feel, and be, more resilient. This is often absent for young people who have moved repeatedly during their childhood, where disruptions of placement result in disruptions to their schooling, to their relationships with their peers and to their position within their extended family. Thus a split can develop between a hurt infant or child part of the adolescent, and a competent, or pseudo–competent, adult part. The latter may involve a defensive reaction to the feelings of despair and helplessness; hope for the future may be located in both the part of the adolescent that is a vulnerable infant and in that post which is genuinely striving to be adult.

Case example: the leaving care team

In a leaving care team, workers became embroiled in a conflict over the methods of work. The problem came to light when only half the team was available to take on new cases. The members of the other half of the team always had full caseloads. In exploring this division, it emerged that two opposing and different approaches were being taken to the work. The group that were available to take on new cases were being reactive to their clients, so that if they requested help, this was provided, but the workers did not seek out those young people who did not themselves ask for help. They also made short-term contracts with the young people, defining work in a task-oriented way. They assumed that young people would find follow-up intrusive. The other team members, in contrast, were proactive in visiting the young people, and were more actively involved in building relationships with the care-leaving adolescents. They felt that their cases were not ready to be closed, and that doors needed to be left open, in case of need. Cases would be followed up for years, rather than weeks.

This split represents different views of vulnerability and need. The short-term model was based on a sense of 'getting on with the present' and making do with resources and limitations as they are. The long-term model included the concept of caring for the infant in the adolescent/young adult, and acting on the fear that the adolescents would not survive without parenting. Within this split are dilemmas, which are not easily reconciled in general terms. The practical needs of young people leaving care (and home) become vital, so that the function of parenting (external and internal) can become represented by commodities. Thus two youth workers who came for consultation about responding to the emotional and mental health needs of homeless young people arrived in a van loaded with a fridge, a cooker and a washing machine. Mothering can be thus reified. Emotional contact can get lost in the emphasis on practicalities, or they can provide opportunities for thinking about meaning and understanding.

Increased homelessness among young people in Britain in the late twentieth century was probably caused by the restructuring of the economy of late adolescence, especially the increased centrality of education, the fragmented routes through late adolescence towards independence, and the extension through these of the period of semi-dependence. The burden of this fell on the most vulnerable, those with extreme family difficulties and those who had already experienced multiple transitions in care. It is a powerful argument that the absence of an internal home, emotionally, stems from the problems in internalising parenting, through its lack, absence, and difficulties, and that this manifests itself as the inability to make a home in the adult world. To move into the adult world after experiences of such damaging quality requires the capacity to take a calculative approach to options, in a context of risks. The experience of contact with someone in a therapeutic role that can bear the anxiety and pain of loss and risks is helpful in keeping together the infant and more adult parts of the adolescent.

Becoming a worker

It is in the arena of becoming an adult worker that great changes have taken place in the context of the late adolescent transition. Young people seeking employment undergo a number of moves involving complex patterns of full-time study, part-time work, part-time study, vocational training, full-time work and unemployment:

> The pattern in Britain is therefore becoming more like that in continental Europe, with young people living with their parents until their late twenties or early thirties, when they are established in work and have some savings. (Joseph Rowntree Foundation 2001)

This requires that families can provide this kind of support and that the young person and the family have sufficiently negotiated their relationships in order to permit this kind of cohabitation.

Some young people are excluded from the opportunities that are available within the complicated routes from school to work. Those who did not reach their potential at school get stuck in low-paid and unrewarding jobs; those who have social difficulties may become long-term unemployed. For many, it is not so much the lack of opportunities but rather the uncertainties that cause the problems. The risks and hazards of the route to work include, probably, a period of unemployment for school-leavers and graduates, requiring the capacity to move between different positions, putting together bits from part-time work and training. The point is not that things are 'worse'. Twenty years ago, two-thirds went straight from school into a full-time job (Joseph Rowntree Foundation 2001), but most of these jobs were in manufacturing industries. The predictability of this route provides few opportunities for change and development. Currently, what typifies transitions is the shift towards unpredictability, and change, and the need for young people to adjust flexibly to different roles – of student, part-time worker, part-time trainee – and to be able to maintain an active pursuit of their future. It is an anxious process.

Erikson (1968) wrote that 'In every technology, and in every historical period there are types of individuals who can combine the dominant techniques with their identity and *become* what they *do*'. This would be a dangerous technique for most young people, who need to be able to move between finite, time-limited and changing conceptions of what they do, in work, and to be able to lose, mourn, relinquish and realign (or, as Giddens puts it, 'reinvent'). The problem, in terms of work identity, is to steer between commitment and flexibility without losing either authenticity or adaptedness. Perhaps this is true of relating as well as working. These requirements demand a great deal of the internal world and the capacity to make sense of experience. Experiences of a flexible and receptive containment in infancy and during adolescence are the prime requirements for young people leaving home, as these provide opportunities to move between different and overlapping subject positions without losing a sense of self, through fragmenting or becoming rigidly stuck in one way of relating to the social world.

Becoming adult

The question that has been avoided is what it means to be adult. The gathering of experience through adolescence leads to participation in an adult world, which is complex, changing, and mirrors, in some ways, adolescence. The turbulence of society means that, in Emery and Trist's phrase, quoted in Chapter 1, 'the ground itself is in motion'. The capacity to maintain authenticity and integrity while changing, and experiencing loss, requires a particular kind of flexibility: the capacity to mourn, and to relinquish, to be introspective and to be aware of destructiveness, the need to repair, where possible, and to face what cannot be repaired; the capacity to bear anxiety and to have a calculative approach to risks. The adult process is not unlike the adolescent process. To Freud's idea that maturity is the capacity to love and work, needs to be added the capacity to weigh risks and bear the consequent anxieties. Thus, it is possibly a useful preparation for adulthood to have an adolescence which has, to a tolerable extent, exposed the individual to the experiences of change and loss. The adolescent may have felt the possibility of fragmentation, and, provided with this awareness may have, through connectedness with others, created a sense of the value of others in performing containing functions for these emotions. Thus self-reflectiveness, an awareness of subjective experiences and inner states of mind, provides possibilities of digesting diverse experiences and making sense of them. An adolescence in which the complexities of relationships are discovered, along with the capacity to love, provides the possibilities of moving between different positions, in which power and vulnerability are reflected upon and experienced. Waddell (1998 p. 175) refers to Bion's view that he worked as a psychoanalyst in order to learn how to become one. This combines the positions of learner and worker, child and adult, apprentice and master, in a reflexive flexibility, which summarises the aliveness and fluidity of the potential and possibilities in the turbulence of modernity. Adolescence provides the opportunities and hazards that follow from the exposure to external and internal turbulence, and the possibilities of making and maintaining a link between immaturity (childhood) and maturity (adulthood). Vulnerabilities and potencies, dependency and learning, independence and agency are linked through the experiences of adolescence and the contact that is made through these different aspects of the self. Through linking childhood experiences and maturity, the importance of the prolonged phase of adolescence is, indeed, immense and vital in so many ways for the achievement of a capacity to contend with the demands of adulthood.

Summary

- Leaving home is a complex and often piecemeal process in contemporary society, and the sequences in which adolescents move into adulthood are diverse, depending very much on context.
- There are special tensions internally in the late adolescent transition, which create a sense of urgency for adolescents. These can be thought of as intensification of the processes of loss and mourning, and of emotional struggles involved in taking up adult positions, in terms of power and vulnerability.
- Some adolescents are particularly vulnerable to the late transition, and risk becoming socially excluded and/or facing unbearable pain. However, case examples have been chosen which illustrate capacities for resilience, sometimes of a surprising nature. These include teenage pregnancy and leaving care.

- Adolescents take up adult positions in terms of work, sexual partnership, and parenting, rather than simply 'leaving home'.
- Since adult society mirrors adolescence to some extent it is a helpful preparation for adulthood to have experiences of change, uncertainty and potential fragmentation, as long as these are tolerable and that containment makes sense of these experiences. This equips adolescents to be flexible *and* authentic at work, and in love.

NOTES

Chapter 1 Contemporary Adolescence: Turbulence or Transition?

1. This refers to Freud's taking the Greek myth of Oedipus to be a cornerstone in individual infantile/childhood development, in which the infant's desire for the opposite-sex parent and competition with the same-sex parent creates a passionate – and bloody – set of 'phantasies'. The 'Oedipus complex' has a number of significant aspects and variations, which, placed in a 'modern' context, as we shall see, have a continuing relevance for understanding development.
2. This refers to Erikson's move to the USA in the wake of Nazi persecution, and the change of his name from 'Homburger'.
3. He used masculine examples throughout *Identity: Youth and Crisis*.
4. The discussion about the late transition is taken up again in Chapter 9, below.
5. Esther Bick described the terror of fragmenting internally in the infant as 'being shot out into outer space without a space suit. The predominant terror of the baby is of falling to pieces or liquefying' (1986 p. 296). Maternal containment has the effect of pulling together the infant within the boundary of the skin, but if the function of providing a 'psychic skin' through containment is disturbed, the infant may make her/his own attempts to hold her/himself together psychically to contend with the terrors of fragmentation. This is described as an omnipotent attempt to replace dependency on others with a pseudo-independent 'second skin'. Becoming wrapped up in clothes may be a way of attempting to provide a second skin. Muscularity and precocious verbal development are others. Adolescents may turn to second skin formation in the absence of understanding, containing figures, who can make sense of the feelings of potential fragmentation.
6. The term 'mother' is meant to be inclusive of any involved care-giver. Technically, the projecting process that originates with the infant is 'projective identification'. Unwanted or overwhelming feelings are split off and projected into the mother, and these parts of the self are then identified with. Perhaps the clearest exposition of this is Klein's (1955) discussion of the novel *If I Were You* by Julian Green, in which the subject, Fabian, envies others more powerful and wealthier than he, and through making a pact with the devil takes over their personalities. The emptiness of the project is revealed when Fabian discovers

that under the sway of his envy he had omitted to take into account the negative aspects of the envied person's life, which he has just inhabited, and a frantic attempt to return follows. Klein (1946) described projective identification as a defensive attempt to omnipotently control the mother/object. Klein thought about degrees of projective identification, in which either parts of the personality or almost all of it, is projected. Bion used the idea of degrees of projective identification to distinguish between a defensive attempt to control the object and a primitive form of communication. The latter is 'normally' used, preverbally, to let another know something of what is felt and experienced, and thus it is a crucial aspect of the container–contained relationship where the mother gets to know her baby by letting her/his feelings enter her. See Hinshelwood 1989 for a further discussion.

Chapter 2 Becoming a Subject in Adolescence

1. Blos's account has some weaknesses in thinking about contemporary adolescence. First, the conceptualising of 'hatching' from fusion to separateness, based on Mahler's (1963) theory of infancy, oversimplifies the relationship processes of both infancy and adolescence. Second, rather like Erikson, Blos places the emphasis on progression towards autonomy and this introduces the idea of a rather solid, unified adult self as an outcome for adolescence.

2. In the paranoid-schizoid position the infant splits the mother, or object, into good, or loved, and bad, or hated, aspects. This is accomplished through projective identification, denial of reality, splitting and idealisation, in order to deal with persecutory anxiety in which the infant is threatened from within by bad, hateful and destructive feelings. The primary aim in the paranoid-schizoid position is to protect the self from difficult, unpleasant and disturbing feelings. In the depressive position the infant becomes more aware of reality and thus that the attacks on the hated object are also attacks on the loved object. In an attempt to make good the damage that it is felt to have been perpetrated on the loved object, there are attempts to make reparation. In the depressive position tolerating ambivalence, pain and concern for the other person is striven for, and if the feelings become unbearable, there results either a return to the paranoid-schizoid position, a retreat into a manic defence, or an overemphasis on guilt, in a masochistic way. In the paranoid-schizoid position, there is no separateness or toleration of separation, and through the projective processes that predominate, the boundaries between self and others are broken through and blurred. In the depressive position, the problem or difficulty is the management of the pain of guilt and separateness, and of the sense of vulnerability that ensues.
The manic defence is important in adolescence. The idea is that to defend against pain and loss, the individual resorts to a denigration of the importance of relationships, and also of dependency, and also that,

omnipotently, everything that has gone wrong can be put right again (see Hinshelwood 1989).
3. See note 1, Chapter 1.
4. Kennedy (2000) makes a similar defining claim: 'subjectivity incorporates both intrapsychic and intersubjective positions, both phenomena within the subject and between subjects in the social field. Psychoanalysis has clarified mainly intrapsychic phenomena, and is only now paying more attention to the intersubjective arena. I am not implying that we should abandon the intrapsychic, for that would be to deny an essential component of the subject' (p. 878).
5. There is a connection with Meltzer's (1988) discussion of the aesthetic conflict. Rustin (1995) has suggested that this is a most radical position:

> This approach views imaginative understanding – conceived as an aesthetic experience of the beautiful and the sublime, in effect – as the true aim of psychic life. It is the encounter with the disturbance of new emotional experience – of which the infant's experience of the breast is for Meltzer the prototype – which creates the possibility of this state of aesthetic apprehension. (p. 240)

6. Bion's term 'the selected fact' had a similar meaning with regard to the internal organisation of the mind.
7. The myth of the 'repressive' hypothesis is for example firmly endorsed by the historian very sympathetic to Freud, Peter Gay (1984).
8. The unity of mind and body, and alternatively, the split between them, Cartesian dualism, is of course a central philosophical theme. Current challenging of the mind–body dualism leads to reconceptualisation of the emotionality of experiences (see, for example, Williams and Bendelow 1998), and a challenging of traditional authorities.
9. Bion (1970) when discussing catastrophic change gives the example of someone trying to control (contain within the self) the intense experience through words, and the failure to do this – through developing a stammer for example. The 'container' is put under excessive pressure in turbulence, and the conditions of catastrophic change. This is close to the idea being discussed here.
10. Irigaray (1991) celebrates the flow and fluidity of femininity. Touch is prioritised over seeing while, taking the labia as a model, she proposes that female sexuality is always plural, always touching herself, without the need for mediation (pp. 204–5). But women's sexuality is 'far more diversified, more multiple in its differences, more complex, more subtle than is commonly imagined' (p. 207).
11. Kristeva is also responsible for developing a concept of 'women's time', which is cyclical, rather than linear.

Chapter 4 Parenting Adolescents

1. Dartington (1998) points out that 'it is not unusual for young people to be quite ruthless in their experimentation at this period' (p. 14).

2. Hinshelwood (1999) develops Freud's conceptualisation that the child internalises not the parent but the parent's super-ego (Freud 1924). In this sense the super-ego conceptualises the way familial and cultural contexts are organised in the mind, through internalisation of parental values, attitudes, norms and prohibitions. The super-ego may have different characteristics, in that it can be a guiding force, even when strict, or it can destructively attack linking and thinking. In this model, the cultural values which are transmitted as unconscious processes are those relating to a socio-cultural state which has past.

Chapter 5 Containing Adolescence in Organisations

1. The term 'institutional defence' was developed by Menzies Lyth (1988).
2. Changes in the organisation of welfare are usually discussed in terms of a shift from a dependency culture to a more competitive one. There are different views on this. Lawrence (1994) has been more optimistic about the changes, in which there is greater involvement and information within organisations, to whom powers have devolved. Lawrence sees the movement in organisations to be away from competition and conflict and towards mutuality. Halton (1995) suggests that some competitiveness within organisations is positive, but that too much emphasis on competition is undermining.

Chapter 6 Adolescents as Temporary Outsiders: Drugs, Offending and Antisocial Behaviour

1. The ideas of transitional space and a potential space for creativity are Winnicott's (1971).
2. The concept of the secure base is Bowlby's (1988). In attachment theory, security of attachment is a prerequisite for the capacity to move away from the parent, and to begin exploratory behaviour. Allen and Land (1999) discuss recent understanding of adolescent attachment behaviour. The absence of a secure base, or of security of attachment, leads to different patterns of relating, based on the distinction between ambivalent/anxious and avoidant responses to separation. Avoidant adolescents tend to try to pull out of emotional engagement, playing down the significance of emotional experiences. Anxious/ambivalent adolescents in contrast make a great deal of all emotional experience, indiscriminately, without prioritising. Thus they make mountains out of molehills, so to speak, while avoidant adolescents, in contrast, make molehills out of mountains.

Chapter 8 Psychotic and Suicidal States in Adolescence

1. The hopelessness of the ego as a key suicide dynamic has been developed by, especially, Beck (for example, Beck *et al.* 1974). The emphasis on hopelessness as a unipolar dynamic can be said to miss

the counterpart – merciless violence and sadism which is found in the super-ego.

2. This is discussed by Campbell (1995) providing a place for the idea of self-preservative violence, as distinct from sado-masochistic excitement (see Perelberg 1999 for a full discussion). Bion's idea of evacuation through massive projective identification is also eliminative.

Chapter 9 Leaving Home

1. The term 'intermediate household' is used in sociological approaches to leaving home (Jones 1995). It has become an increasingly common form of transition, affecting both middle- and working-class young people, though the type of accommodation may be different. Middle-class young adults live in shared student or post-student accommodation; working-class young adults live in hostels, or board with relatives or in accommodation provided by employers (Furlong and Cartmel 1997).

BIBLIOGRAPHY

Achenbach, T., Howell, C., McConaughty, S., and Stanger, C. (1998) 'Six-year predictors of problems in a national sample: IV. Young adult signs of disturbance', *Journal of the American Academy of Child and Adolescent Psychiatry*, 37, 718–27.

Alexander, C. (2000) '(Dis)Entangling the "asian gang": ethnicity, identity, masculinity', in Hesse, B. (ed.), *Un/settled Multiculturalisms* (London: Jed Books).

Allen, J. and Land, P. (1999) 'Attachment in adolescence', in Cassidy, J. and Shaver, P. (eds), *Handbook of Attachment – Theory, Research and Clinical Implications* (New York: Guilford Press).

Ambrose, M. (2001) 'The developmental and emotional implications behind the use young people make of family planning services', in Baruch, G. (ed.), *Community Based Psychotherapy with Young People: Evidence and Innovation in Practice* (Hove: Brunner-Routledge).

Amiel, O. (2001) 'Why come, why come back; developing and maintaining a long term therapeutic alliance with young people who have had a psychotic breakdown', in Baruch, G. (ed.), *Community Based Psychotherapy with Young People: Evidence and Innovation in Practice* (Hove: Brunner-Routledge).

Anderson, R. (1997) 'Putting the boot in. Violent defences against depressive anxiety', in Bell, D. (ed.), *Reason and Passion. A Celebration of the Work of Hanna Segal* (London: Duckworth/Tavistock Clinic Series).

Anderson, R. (1999) 'Introduction', in Anastasopoulos, D., Laylou-Lignos, E. and Waddell M. (eds), *Psychoanalytic Psychotherapy of the Severely Disturbed Adolescent* (London: Karnac Books).

Anderson, R. and Dartington, A. (1998) *Facing It Out: Clinical Perspectives on Adolescent Disturbance* (London: Duckworth/Tavistock Clinic Series).

Back, L. (1997) 'Pale shadows': racisms, masculinity and multiculture', in Roche, J. and Tucker, S. (eds), *Youth in Society* (London: Sage).

Bains, R. (2001) 'Psychotherapy with young people from ethnic minority backgrounds in different community based settings', in Baruch, G. (ed.), *Community Based Psychotherapy with Young People: Evidence and Innovation in Practice* (Hove: Brunner-Routledge).

Baruch, G. (ed.) (2001) *Community Based Psychotherapy with Young People: Evidence and Innovation in Practice* (Hove: Brunner-Routledge).

Beck, A., Schuyler, D., and Herman, A. (1974) 'Development of suicidal intent scales' in Beck, A., Resnick, H. and Lettieri, D. (eds), *The Prediction of Suicide* (Charles Press: Bowie, Maryland).

Beck, U. (1992) *Risk Society: Towards a New Modernity* (London: Sage).

Beck-Gernsheim, E. (1998) 'On the way to a post-familial family: from a community of need to elective affinities', *Theory, Culture and Society*, *15*(3–4), 53–70.

Bell, D. (2000) 'Who is killing what or whom? Some notes on the internal phenomenology of suicide', *Psychoanalytic Psychotherapy*, *15*(1), 21–37.

Bhabha, H. (1990) *Nation and Narration* (London: Routledge).

Bhabha, H. (1997) 'Culture's in Between', in Bennett, D. (ed.), *Multicultural States – Rethinking Difference and Identity* (London: Routledge).

Bhattacharyya, G. and Gabriel, J. (1997) 'Racial formations in youth in late twentieth century England', in Roche, J. and Tucker, S. (eds), *Youth in Society* (London: Sage).

Bick, E. (1968) 'The experience of the skin in early object relationships', *International Journal of Psychoanalysis*, *49*, 484–6.

Bick, E. (1986) 'Further considerations of the function of the skin in early object relations: findings from infant observation integrated into child and adult analysis', *British Journal of Psychotherapy*, *2*(4), 292–301.

Bion, W. (1962) *Learning From Experience* (London: Maresfield).

Bion, W. (1963) *Elements of Psychoanalysis* (London: Maresfield).

Bion, W. (1970) *Attention and Interpretation* (London: Maresfield).

Blos, P. (1962) *On Adolescence: a psychoanalytic interpretation* (New York: Free Press of Glencoe).

Blos, P. (1967) 'The second individuation process of adolescence', *Psychoanalytic Study of the Child*, *22*, 162–86.

Blos, P. (1984) 'Son and father', *Journal of the American Psychoanalytic Association*, *32*, 301–24.

Bollas, C. (1991) *Forces of Destiny: Psychoanalysis and Human Idiom* (London: Free Association Books).

Bordo, S. (1993) *Unbearable Weight* (Berkeley: University of California Press).

Bowlby, J. A. (1988) *Secure Base. Clinical Applications of Attachment Theory* (London: Routledge).

Bowley, J. (1996) 'Survival at the front: A study of the Work of the Nursing Staff in an Adolescent Psychiatric Unit', MA dissertation, Tavistock Clinic/University of East London.

Brah, A. (1996) *Cartographies of Diaspora* (London: Routledge).

Brenman Pick, I. (1988) 'Adolescence: its impact on patient and analyst', *International Journal of Psychoanalysis*, *15*, 187.

Briggs, S. (1995) 'Parallel process: emotional and physical digestion in adolescents with eating disorders', *Journal of Social Work Practice*, *9*(2), 155–68.

Briggs, S. (1997) *Growth and Risk in Infancy* (London: Jessica Kingsley).

Britton, R. (1989) 'The missing link: parental sexuality in the Oedipus complex', in Steiner, J. (ed.), *The Oedipus Complex Today* (London: Karnac Books).

Britton, R. (1998) *Belief and Imagination: Explorations in Psychoanalysis* (London: Routledge).

Buytendijk, F. (1974) *Prolegomena to an Anthropological Physiology* (Pittsburgh: Duquesne University Press).

Cahn, R. (1998) 'The process of becoming-a-subject in adolescence', in Perret-Catipovic, M. and Ladame, F. (eds), *Adolescence and Psychoanalysis: The Story and the History* (London: Karnac Books).

Campbell, D. (1995) 'The role of the father in a pre-suicide state', *International Journal of Psycho-analysis*, 76(2), 315–23.

Campbell, D. and Hale, R. (1991) 'Suicidal acts', in Holmes, J. (ed.), *Textbook of Psychotherapy in Psychiatric Practice* (London: Churchill Livingstone).

Chodorow, N. (1995) 'Individuality and difference in how women and men love', in Elliott, A. and Frosh, S. (eds), *Psychoanalysis in Contexts* (London: Routledge).

Cohen, S. (1993) *Folk Devils and Moral Panics* (London: McGibbon & Kee).

Coleman, J. and Hendry, L. (1999) *The Nature of Adolescence*, 3rd edn (London: Routledge).

Cooper, A. (2000) 'The state of mind we're in', *Soundings*, 3(1), 118–38.

Dale, F. (1991) 'The Art of Communicating with Vulnerable Children', in Varma, V. (ed.), *The Secret Life of Vulnerable Children* (London: Routledge).

Dartington, A. (1994) 'Some thoughts on the significance of the outsider in families and other social groups', in Box, S. (ed.), *Crisis at Adolescence: Object Relations Therapy with the Family* (New York: Jason Aronson).

Dartington, A. (1998) 'The intensity of adolescence in small families', in Anderson, R. and Dartington, A. (eds), *Facing it Out; Clinical Perspectives on Adolescent Disturbance* (London: Duckworth/Tavistock Clinic Series).

Dubinsky, H. (1999) 'Factors Contributing to the Psychotic Breakdown of Three Adolescents', in Anastasopoulos, D., Laylou-Lignos, E. and Waddell, M. (eds), *Psychoanalytic Psychotherapy of the Severely Disturbed Adolescent* (London: Karnac Books).

Edwards, T. (1997) 'Sexuality', in Roche, J. and Tucker, S. *Youth in Society* (London: Sage).

Eisenbruch, M. (1990) 'Cultural bereavement and homesickness', in Fisher, S. and Cooper, C.L. (eds), *On the Move: The Psychology of Change and Transition* (Chichester: Wiley).

Emery, F. and Trist, E. (1969) 'The causal texture of organisational environments', in Emery, F. (ed.), *Systems Thinking* (Harmondsworth: Penguin).

Erikson, E. (1968) *Identity: Youth and Crisis* (London: Faber).

Flynn, D. (2000) 'Adolescence', in Wise, I. (ed.), *Adolescence* (London: Institute of Psychoanalysis).

Fonagy, P. and Target, M. (1999) 'Towards understanding violence: the use of the body and the role of the father', in Perelberg, R. (ed.), *Psychoanalytic Understanding of Violence and Suicide* (London: Routledge).

Foucault, M. (1977) *Discipline and Punish* (London: Peregrine).

Foucault, M. (1979, 1984a, 1984b) *The History of Sexuality*, volumes I–III (London: Penguin).

Foucault, M. (1988) 'Technologies of the self', in Martin, L., Gutman, H. and Hutton, P. (eds), *Technologies of the Self: a Seminar with Michel Foucault* (London: Tavistock).

French, S. and Swain, J. (1997) 'Young disabled people', in Roche, J. and Tucker, S. (eds), *Youth in Society* (London: Sage Publications).

Freud, S. (1916) 'Some character types met with in psycho-analytic work', in Strachy, J. (ed.), *The Standard Edition of the Complete Psychological Works of Sigmund Freud*, vol. 14 (London: The Hogarth Press and the Institute of Psychoanalysis).

Freud, S. (1917) 'Mourning and melancholia', in Strachey, J. (ed.), *The Standard Edition of the Complete Psychological Works of Sigmund Freud*, vol. 14 (London: Hogarth Press and the Institute of Psychoanalysis).

Freud, S. (1920) 'The psychogenesis of a case of female homosexuality', in Strachey, J. (ed.), *The Standard Edition of the Complete Psychological Works of Sigmund Freud*, vol. 18 (London: Hogarth Press and the Institute of Psychoanalysis).

Freud, S. (1923) 'The ego and the id', in Strachey, J. (ed.), *The Standard Edition of the Complete Psychological Works of Sigmund Freud*, vol. 19 (London: Hogarth Press and the Institute of Psychoanalysis).

Freud, S. (1924) 'The economic problem of masochism', in Strachey, J. (ed.), *The Standard Edition of the Complete Psychological Works of Sigmund Freud*, vol. 19 (London: Hogarth Press and the Institute of Psychoanalysis).

Frosh, S. (1991) *Identity Crisis: Modernity, Psychoanalysis and the Self* (London: Macmillan).

Furlong, A. and Cartmel, F. (1997) *Young People and Social Change; Individualisation and Risk in Modern Society* (Buckingham: Open University Press).

Garnett, L. (1992) *Leaving Care and After* (London: National Children's Bureau).

Gay, P. (1984) *The Bourgeois Experience: From Victoria to Freud. Volume 1 – Education of the Senses* (Oxford: Oxford University Press).

Ghuman, P.A. (1999) Singh. *Asian Adolescents in the West* (Leicester: British Psychological Society Books).

Giddens, A. (1991) *Modernity and Self-Identity* (Oxford: Polity Press).

Graham, P. (1986) 'Behavioural and Intellectual Development in Childhood Epidemiology', *British Medical Bulletin*, 42, 155–62.

Green, A. (1992) 'A psychoanalyst's point of view concerning psychosis at adolescence', in Schwartzberg, A. (ed.), *International Annals of Adolescent Psychiatry* (Chicago: University of Chicago Press).

Greenberg, H. (1975) 'The widening gyre: transformations of the omnipotent quest during adolescence', *International Review of Psychoanalysis*, *2*, 231–44.

Griffin, C. (1997) 'Representations of the Young', in Roche, J. and Tucker, S. (eds), *Youth in Society* (London: Sage Publications).

Habermas, J. (1994) 'Struggle for recognition in the democratic constitutional state', in Gutman, A. (ed.), *Multiculturalism* (Princeton, NJ: Princeton University Press).

Hall, S. (1988) *Hard Road to Renewal* (London: Verso).

Hall, S. (2000) 'Conclusion: the multi-cultural question', in Hesse, B. (ed.), *Un/settled Multiculturalisms* (London: Jed Books).

Halton, W. (1995) 'Institutional stress on providers of health and education', *Psychodynamic Counselling*, *1*(2), 187–98.

Heimann, P. (1995) 'On countertransference', *International Journal of Psychoanalysis*, *31*, 81–4.

Hinshelwood, R. (1989) *A Dictionary of Kleinian Thought* (London: Free Association Books).

Hinshelwood, R. (1999) 'Identity and some psychoanalytic implications', *Journal of Melanie Klein and Object Relations*, *17*(1), 149–60.

Hollway, W. (1989) *Subjectivity and Method in Psychology* (London: Sage).

Hollway, W. and Jefferson, T. (2000) *Doing Qualitative Research Differently; Free Association, Narrative and the Interview Method* (London: Sage).

Hoxter, S. (1964) 'The experience of puberty'. *Journal of Child Psychotherapy*, *1*(2), 13–26.

Irigaray, L. (1991) 'This sex which is not one', in Gunew, S. (ed.), *Feminist Knowledge: A Reader* (London: Routledge).

Jacobs, T. (1990) 'The no age time: early adolescence and its consequences', in Dowling, S. (ed.), *Child and Adolescent Analysis: Its Significance for Clinical Work* (Madison, CT: International Universities Press).

Jones, E. (1922) 'Some Problems of Adolescence', *British Journal of Psychology*, *13*, 31–47.

Jones, G. (1995) *Leaving Home* (Buckingham: Open University Press).

Joseph Rowntree Foundation (2001) *Young Men on the Margins of Work: Findings* (York: Joseph Rowntree Foundation).

Kennedy, R. (1998) *The Elusive Human Subject: A Psychoanalytic Theory of Subject Relations* (London: Free Association Books).

Kennedy, R. (2000) 'Becoming a Subject: Some Theoretical and Clinical Issues', *International Journal of Psychoanalysis*, *81*, 875–92.

Klein, M. (1935) 'A Contribution to the Psychogenesis of Manic-depressive States', in Klein M. (ed.), *Love, Guilt and Reparation and Other Works* (London: Hogarth).

Klein, M. (1922) 'On Puberty', in Klein, M. (ed.), *Love, Guilt and Reparation and Other Works* (London: Hogarth Press, 1975).

Klein, M. (1946) 'Notes on some Schizoid mechanisms', in Klein, M. (ed.), *Envy and Gratitude and Other Works* (London: Hogarth, 1975).

Klein, M. (1955) 'On identification', in Klein, M. (ed.), *Envy and Gratitude and Other Works* (London: Hogarth, 1975).

Kristeva, J. (1982) *Powers of Horror: An Essay on Abjection* (New York: Columbia University Press).

Ladame, F. (2001) 'Treatment of suicidal adolescents', Conference Paper, Suicidality and Psychoanalysis, 30 August–2 September 2001, Hamburg.

Lash, S. (1999) *Sociology of Post-Modernism* (London: Routledge).

Laufer, M. and Laufer, E. (1984) *Adolescence and Developmental Breakdown* (London: Karnac).

Laufer, E. (1985) 'Loss of the sense of reality about death', in Laufer, M. (ed.), *The Suicidal Adolescent* (London: Karnac).

Lawrence, G. (1994) *The Politics of Salvation and the Politics of Revelation: What Makes Consultancy Work?* (London: South Bank University Press).

Lawrence, M. (2001) 'Loving them to death: the anorexic and her objects', *International Journal of Psychoanalysis*, 82, 43–55.

Lowe, F. (2001) Personal communication.

Magagna, J. (2000) 'Severe eating difficulties: attacks on life', in Rustin, M.E. and Quagliata, E. (eds), *Assessment in Child Psychotherapy* (London: Duckworth/Tavistock Clinic Series).

Mahler, M. (1963) 'Thoughts about development and individuation', *Psychoanalytic Study of the Child*, 8, 307–24.

Mak-Pearce, G. (2001) 'Engaging troubled adolescents in six session psychodynamic therapy', in Baruch, G. (ed.), *Community Based Psychotherapy with Young People: Evidence and Innovation in Practice* (Hove: Brunner-Routledge).

Martin, B. (1981) *A Sociology of Contemporary Popular Culture* (Oxford: Blackwell).

Mawson, C. (1994) 'Containing anxiety in work with damaged children', in Obholzer, A. and Roberts, V. (eds), *The Unconscious at Work* (London: Routledge).

McDougall, J. (1986) *Theatre of the Body* (London: Free Association Books).

Meltzer, D. and Harris Williams, M. (1988) *The Apprehension of Beauty: The Role of Aesthetic Conflict in Development, Art and Violence* (Strath Tay: Clunie Press).

Menzies Lyth, I. (1988) *The Dynamics of the Social: Selected Essays*, vol. 2 (London: Free Association Books).

Miller, L. (1998) 'Psychotherapy with learning disabled adolescents', in Anderson, R. and Dartington, A. (eds), *Facing It Out: Clinical Perspectives on Adolescent Disturbance* (London: Duckworth/Tavistock Clinic Series).

Musick, J. (1993) *Young, Poor and Pregnant; The Psychology of Teenage Parenthood* (New Howen, CT: Yale University Press).

Noam, G. (1999) 'The psychology of belonging. Reformulating adolescent development', in Esman, A. and Flaherty, L. (eds), *Adolescent Psychiatry; Development and Clinical Studies*, vol. 24.

Parekh, B. (1991) 'British citizenship and cultural difference', in Andrews, G. (ed.), *Citizenship* (London: Lawrence & Wishart).

Parker, D. (2000) 'The Chinese takeaway and the diasporic habitus: space, time and power geometrics', in Hesse, B. (ed.), *Unsettled Multiculturalisms* (London: Jed Books).

Perret-Catipovic, M. and Ladame, F. (1998) *Adolescence and Psychoanalysis: The Story and the History* (London: Karnac Books).

Phoenix, A. (1991) *Young Mothers* (Oxford: Polity Press).

Pini, M. (1997) 'Technologies of the self', in Roche, J. and Tucker, S. (eds), *Youth in Society* (London: Sage).

Plaut, E. and Hutchinson, F. (1986) 'The role of puberty in female psychosexual development', *International Review of Psychoanalysis*, *13*, 417–32.

Prendergast, S. (1995) 'With gender on my mind: menstruation and embodiment at adolescence', in Holland, J., Blair, M. and Sheldon, S. (eds), *Debates and Issues in Feminist Research and Pedagogy* (Buckingham: Open University Press).

Radonic, Z. (2001) 'The clinician's experience of implementing audit and its impact on the clinical process in the treatment of troubled young people', in Baruch, G. (ed.), *Community-Based Psychotherapy with Young People: Evidence and Innovation in Practice* (Hove: Brunner-Routledge).

Roberts, K. (1995) *Youth and Employment in Modern Britain* (Oxford University Press).

Roche, J. and Tucker, S. (eds) (1997) *Youth in Society* (London: Sage).

Rodriguez de la Sierra, L. (2000) 'Working with addicts', in Wise, I. (ed.), *Adolescence* (London: Institute of Psychoanalysis).

Rosenfeld, H. (1987) *Impasse and Interpretation* (London: Tavistock).

Rustin, M.E. (2000) 'What follows family breakdown? Assessing children who have experienced deprivation, trauma and multiple loss', in Rustin, M.E. and Quagliata, E. (eds), *Assessment in Child Psychotherapy* (London: Duckworth/Tavistock Clinic Series).

Rustin, M.J. (1991) *The Good Society and the Inner World* (London: Verso).

Rustin, M.J. (1995) 'Lacan, Klein and politics: the positive and negative in psychoanalytic thought', in Elliott, A. and Frosh, S. (eds), *Psychoanalysis in Contexts* (London: Routledge).

Sacks, O. (1986) *The Man Who Mistook His Wife for a Hat* (London: Picador).

Sayers, J. (1991) *Boy Crazy: Remembering Adolescence, Therapies and Dreams* (London: Routledge).

Segal, H. (1995) 'From Hiroshima to the Gulf War and After', in Elliott, A. and Frosh, S. (eds), *Psychoanalysis in Contexts* (London: Routledge).

Smith, D. and Rutter, M. (eds) (1995) *Psychosocial Disorders in Young People: Time Trends and Their Causes*. (Chichester: John Wiley).

Sours, J. (1981) *Starving to Death in a Sea of Objects* (New York: Aronson).

Srinath, S. (1998) 'Identificatory processes in trauma', in Garland, C. (ed.), *Understanding Trauma: A Psychoanalytic Approach* (London: Duckworth/Tavistock Clinic Series).

Steiner J. (1993) *Psychic Retreats* (London: Routledge).

Stern, D. (1985) *The Interpersonal World of the Infant* (New York: Basic Books).

Tan, R. (1993) 'Racism and similarity: paranoid-schizoid structures', *British Journal of Psychotherapy*, *10*(1), 33–43.

Tremain, R. (1998) *The Way I Found Her* (London: Vintage).

Trevatt, D. (2001) 'Working in a school for severely physically disabled children', in Baruch, G. (ed.), *Community-Based Psychotherapy with Young People: Evidence and Innovation in Practice* (Hove: Brunner-Routledge).

Urwin, C. (1998) 'Power relations and the emergence of language', in Henriques, J., Hollway, W. and Urwin, C. (eds), *Changing the Subject: Psychology, Social Regulation and Subjectivity*, 3rd edn (London: Routledge).

Van Heeswyk, P. (1997) *Analysing Adolescence* (London: Sheldon Press).

Waddell, M. (1998) *Inside Lives: Psychoanalysis and the Growth of the Personality* (London: Duckworth/Tavistock Clinic Series).

Watson, D. and West, J. (2001) 'Managing change in residential child care', *Journal of Social Work Practice 15*(1), 91–101.

Wiener J. and Sher, M. (1998) *Counselling and Psychotherapy in Primary Health Care: A Psychodynamic Approach* (Basingstoke: Macmillan).

Williams, A.H. (1978) 'Depression, deviation and acting-out in adolescence', *Journal of Adolescence*, *1*, 309–17.

Williams, A.H. (1998) *Cruelty, Violence and Murder: Understanding the Criminal Mind* (London: Karnac).

Williams, G. (1997) *Internal Landscapes and Foreign Bodies* (London: Duckworth/Tavistock Clinic Series).

Williams, G. (2001) 'Work with parents of psychotic children or adolescents', EFPP Conference, Caen.

Williams, S. and Bendelow, G. (1998) *The Lived Body: Sociological Themes, Embodied Issues* (London: Routledge).

Wilson, P. (1996) 'The anti-social tendency', *Journal of Child Psychotherapy*, *22*(3), 394–98.

Winnicott, D. (1971) *Playing and Reality* (Harmondsworth: Pelican).

Wise, I. (2000) *Adolescence* (London: Institute of Psychoanalysis).

Young, L. and Gibb, E. (1998) 'Trauma and grievance', in Garland, C. (ed.), *Understanding Trauma: A Psychoanalytic Approach* (London: Duckworth/Tavistock Clinic Series).

INDEX